VIDEO ON DEMAND SYSTEMS
Technology, Interoperability and Trials

edited by

Shih-Fu Chang
Dimitris Anastassiou
Alexandros Eleftheriadis
John V. Pavlik
Columbia University

A Special Issue of
MULTIMEDIA TOOLS AND APPLICATIONS
An International Journal
Volume 5, No. 2 (1997)

SPRINGER SCIENCE+BUSINESS MEDIA, LLC

MULTIMEDIA TOOLS AND APPLICATIONS

An International Journal

Volume 5, No. 2, September 1997

Special Issue on Video on Demand Systems: Technology, Interoperability, and Trials
Guest Editors: Shih-Fu Chang, Dimitris Anastassiou, Alexandros Eleftheriadis and John V. Pavlik

Library of Congress Cataloging-in-Publication Data

Video on demand systems : technology, interoperability, and trials / edited by Shih-Fu Chang ... [et al.].
p. cm.
"A special issue of Multimedia tools and applications, an international journal, volume 5, no. 2 (1997)."
Includes bibliographical references.
ISBN 978-1-4757-8281-3 ISBN 978-0-585-28766-9 (eBook)
DOI 10.1007/978-0-585-28766-9
1. Multimedia systems. 2. Video recordings. I. Chang, Shih Fu, 1963- . II. Multimedia tools and applications. Special issue.
QA76.575.V525 1997
384.55--dc21 97-17632
CIP

Originally published by Kluwer Academic Publishers in 1997
Softcover reprint of the hardcover 1st edition 1997

Printed on acid-free paper.

Multimedia Tools and Applications 5, 115–118 (1997)

Guest Editorial

Columbia University hosted the 13th meeting of the Digital Audio-Visual Council (DAVIC) on June 17–21, 1996, in New York City. During the meeting, several Video-on-Demand (VoD) groups from around the world participated in a DAVIC annex event for VoD interoperability demonstrations. In addition, a workshop was held on June 24th to provide a dedicated forum for VoD researchers and application developers to exchange their knowledge and experience. This workshop drew an enthusiastic response from a large group of participants from different countries and various technical disciplines, including media companies. Several VoD groups presented technical architectures and design strategies of their testbeds, along with interactive demos in a special demo session.

This special issue of the MTAP journal consists of extended versions of selected workshop presentations. We feel that the workshop program possessed several unique features that are of value to the general technical and scientific community: it included participation from leading research groups working on large-scale VoD and interactive TV testbed development; all participating groups either have developed large-scale VoD system or have experience in actual VoD field trials; finally, it also includes presentations by leading authorities in media and content production companies.

As indicated by the title, this special issue consists of three tracks: (1) Testbed and DAVIC Interoperability, (2) VoD and Interactive TV Trials, and (3) Applications and Content Providers. Each track has representative articles contributed by groups that participated in the VoD workshop. The first track includes articles describing significant efforts in testbed development and interoperability experiments. It includes balanced samples of efforts in industry, academia, and government laboratories. The second track focuses on actual ongoing field trials. Two articles describe international trials of VoD and interactive services using DAVIC compliant technologies. The third track focuses on applications and content providers. With two insightful articles from media company representatives, it serves as a complement to the technical theme of the first two tracks: it brings out unique view points and perspectives from experts with substantial experience in development of new media applications and products.

It should be noted that most VoD systems described in this special issue were partially or entirely based on the DAVIC specifications. In particular, the spirit of interoperability was highlighted in a dedicated session on Interoperability Demonstrations. In order to provide a brief overview of the DAVIC objectives and specifications, we provide an introductory article suitable for a general audience.

Video on demand is a critical enabling technology for many exciting new media applications. Although there has been some set back in terms of the speed of large scale deployment due to economic concern and uncertainty of market trends, intensive interest and R&D work continue in various sectors and disciplines. At Columbia University, pilot applications have been initiated for an Electronic News Service, Courses on Demand,

Mobile Journalist Terminals, and other new media applications. Everyday we also read about new products and ventures in this area, employing a rich variety of technologies. We hope this special issue will provide useful information to the MTAP readership, and will highlight solutions for the several difficult engineering problems entailed in bringing these new technologies and applications to reality.

We would like to thank the following colleagues for their help in manuscript review:

Mahesh Balakrishnan, Andrew Campbell, Tzi-cker Chiueh, Benjamin Compaine, Albert Greco, Steve Jacobs, Hari Kalva, Alexander Loui, Max Ott, Giovanni Pacifici, Adam Powell, Frederick Williams.

Finally, we would like to thank the Editor in Chief of the MTAP journal, Prof. Borko Furht, for his invitation to organize this special issue. Thanks are also due to the editorial staff of Kluwer Academic Publishers, particularly Mr. Bob Holland and Ms. Melissa Fearon.

Shih-Fu Chang
Dept. of Electrical Engineering
Dimitris Anastassiou
Dept. of Electrical Engineering
Alexandros Eleftheriadis
Dept. of Electrical Engineering
John V. Pavlik
Graduate School of Journalism, Columbia University

Shih-Fu Chang is currently an Associate Professor at Department of Electrical Engineering and Center for Telecommunications Research in Columbia University. He received the M.S. and Ph.D. degree in Electrical Engineering and Computer Science from the University of California at Berkeley in 1991 and 1993, respectively.

Dr. Chang's current research interests include content-based image technologies for multimedia systems, visual information systems, and image/video signal processing and communications. At Columbia, he is co-leading the development of a Video-on-Demand/Multimedia Testbed, and Columbia's audio-visual service interoperability experiments. His group has developed several advanced prototypes in visual information systems, including an image/video search and cataloging engine, WebSEEk, and a Web-based compressed video editing and search system, Web Clip.

He was the recipient of the best paper award of SPIE International Symposium on Visual Communications and Image Processing 1995, the best student paper award of the ACM first Multimedia Conference 1993, an NSF CAREER award 1995–8, and an IBM University Research Partnership (Faculty Development) Award 1995–8. He serves on the editorial boards and program committees of several international conferences and publications. He was the organizer and co-chair of Workshop on Video on Demand Systems—Technology, Interoperability and Trials, held at Columbia University in June 1996.

Dimitris Anastassiou was born in Athens, Greece, in 1952. He received the Diploma in electrical engineering from the National Technical University of Athens, Greece, in 1974, and the M.S. and Ph.D. degrees from the University of California, Berkeley, in 1975 and 1979, respectively.

He joined the faculty of Columbia University in 1983, where he is currently Professor of Electrical Engineering, Director of the Image and Advanced Television Laboratory, and Director of Columbia University's cross-disciplinary "New Media Technology Center".

Prior to joining Columbia University in 1983, he was with the IBM Thomas J. Watson Research Center, Yorktown Heights, NY, as a Research Staff Member, working on the development of the internal IBM videoconferencing system.

His research interests focus on digital video processing and communications, with emphasis on multimedia applications. He has received an IBM Outstanding Innovation Award and an NSF Presidential Young Investigator Award. He is an Associate Editor of the IEEE Transactions on Circuits and Systems for Video Technology, and a member of ISO's Moving Picture Experts Group (MPEG) digital video coding standardization effort. He has been Guest Editor of special issues for various journals and has co-organized MPEG and DAVIC meetings at Columbia University, as well as several workshops and sessions on the subject of digital video and Advanced Television.

Alexandros Eleftheriadis was born in Athens, Greece, in 1967. He received the Diploma in Electrical Engineering and Computer Science from the National Technical University of Athens, Greece, in 1990, and the M.S., M.Phil., and Ph.D. degrees in Electrical Engineering from Columbia University, New York, in 1992, 1994, and 1995 respectively.

Since 1995 he has been an Assistant Professor in the Department of Electrical Engineering at Columbia University, where he is leading a research team working in the areas of video signal processing and compression, video communication systems, distributed multimedia systems, and the fundamentals of compression. During the summers of 1993 and 1994, he was with AT&T Bell Laboratories, Murray Hill, NJ, developing low bit rate video coding techniques for videoconferencing applications. From 1990 until 1995, he was a Graduate Research Assistant in the Department of Electrical Engineering at Columbia University.

Prof. Eleftheriadis is a member of the ANSI X3L3.1 Committee, and is participating in the ISO/IEC JTC1/SC29/WG11 (MPEG) standardization activity as well as DAVIC. He is also a member of the IEEE, the ACM, and the Technical Chamber of Greece.

John V. Pavlik is the executive director of The Center for New Media at the Columbia University Graduate School of Journalism, where he is also a professor. Pavlik is also a senior fellow at the San Diego Supercomputer Center, one of four national supercomputer centers funded by the National Science Foundation. Previously, he served as the founding director of the School of Communication at San Diego State University. He is the former associate director for Research and Technology Studies at The Freedom Forum Media Studies Center.

Pavlik most-recent articles are "Competition: Key to the Communications Future?" and "Television News: A Crisis of Opportunity", published in Television Quarterly (Volume 28, Numbers 1 and 2), and "New Media Offer Growing Job Prospects", Nieman Reports, Summer, 1996. His books include New Media Technology, published in 1996 by Allyn & Bacon.

Multimedia Tools and Applications 5, 119–132 (1997)

DAVIC and Interoperability Experiments

HARI KALVA hari@itnm.columbia.edu
SHIH-FU CHANG sfchang@itnm.columbia.edu
ALEXANDROS ELEFTHERIADIS eleft@itnm.columbia.edu
Image and Advanced Television Laboratory, Department of Electrical Engineering, Columbia University, New York, NY 10027, USA

Abstract. To promote the development and deployment of broadband audio visual services, DAVIC has been working on specifying the standards and interfaces for end-to-end systems providing services to consumers over broadband networks. DAVIC specifies tools to provide these broadband services. Since the tools specified by DAVIC are standardized/developed by independent organizations, it is important to verify that the complete system works when these tools are used together. An interoperability event was organized by Columbia University for this very purpose. In this paper we first introduce DAVIC and DAVIC systems and then give details of the interoperability event: the motivation, goals, and results.

Keywords: DAVIC, multimedia standardization, interoperability

1. Introduction to DAVIC

The Digital Audio Visual Council (DAVIC) is a consortium of companies, research institutes, and universities standardizing tools for end-to-end systems to provide broadband audio visual services [5, 8]. DAVIC was established in June 1994 and following an aggressive schedule, released the first specification, DAVIC 1.0 in December 1995. DAVIC 1.0 specifies the tools for the basic DAVIC system. DAVIC is continuing its work by specifying extensions to the specification. The first extension, DAVIC 1.1, was released in September 1996, and the second extension, DAVIC 1.2, will be released in December 1996. DAVIC for the most part picks existing standards for its specifications. However, if a standard does not exist for a particular technology, DAVIC creates a new standard. The following table shows some of the technologies selected by DAVIC for the 1.0 specification.

DAVIC systems are expected to support a wide range of applications. DAVIC has identified 19 core applications and prioritized them based on interest. Some of the intended applications are, movies on demand, tele-shopping, broadcast, games, karoke on demand, tele-work, and news on demand.

Figure 1 shows the reference model of a DAVIC system. The figure shows the reference points in the system and the interfaces between the sub-systems at these reference points. Reference points assume importance in a DAVIC system as a compliant implementation needs to be compliant only at these reference points. The information flow between the sub-systems is divided into five flows, S1 through S5. S1 information flow corresponds to the principal service information, e.g., MPEG-2 transport stream carrying audio and video. The S2 flow corresponds to the user control information, S3 corresponds to session control, S4

Table 1. Technologies chosen in DAVIC 1.0.

Tool	Technology
Video	MPEG-2, MP@ML (ISO/IEC 13818-2)
Audio	MPEG-1 (ISO/IEC 11172-3)
Core network	ATM
Access network	FTTH, FTTC, broadcast, ADSL, HFC ...
User control	DSMCC-UU (ISO 13818-6)
Session control	DSMCC-UU (ISO 13818-6)
Connection control	Q.2931 (CCITT/ITU-T Q.2931)

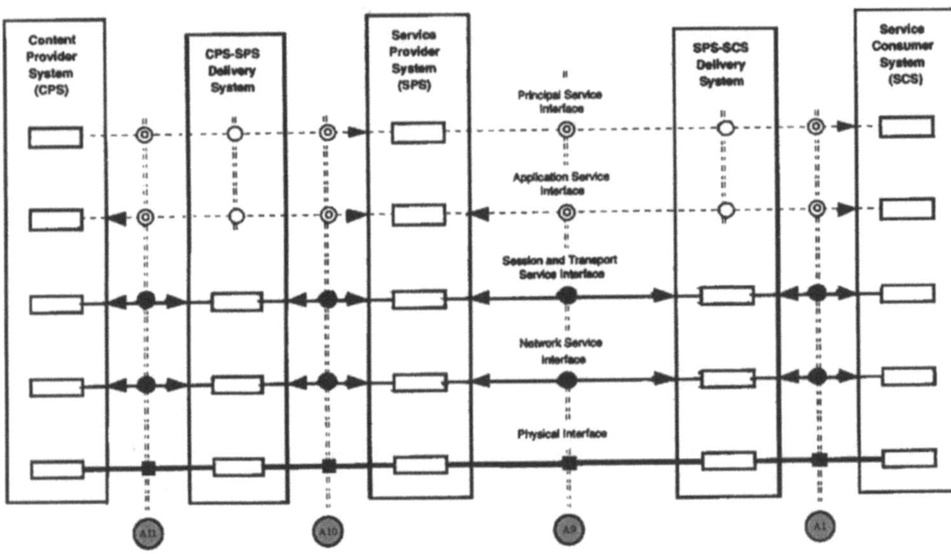

Figure 1. DAVIC reference model [8].

to connection management, and S5 corresponds to billing and other management functions. The S1 flow is unidirectional from the service provider to the service consumer (STU) in DAVIC 1.0 while the other information flows are bidirectional. Future versions of the specification are expected to include a bidirectional S1 flow supporting applications such as video conferencing. The five logical information flows may use a single physical channel or more than one physical channel. In the following sub-sections, a brief description of the components of a DAVIC system is given.

1.1. Service consumer system (SCS)

SCS is another terminology for customer premise equipment (CPE) and usually consists of a NIU, an STU, a display terminal such as a TV, and other peripherals. The SCS is

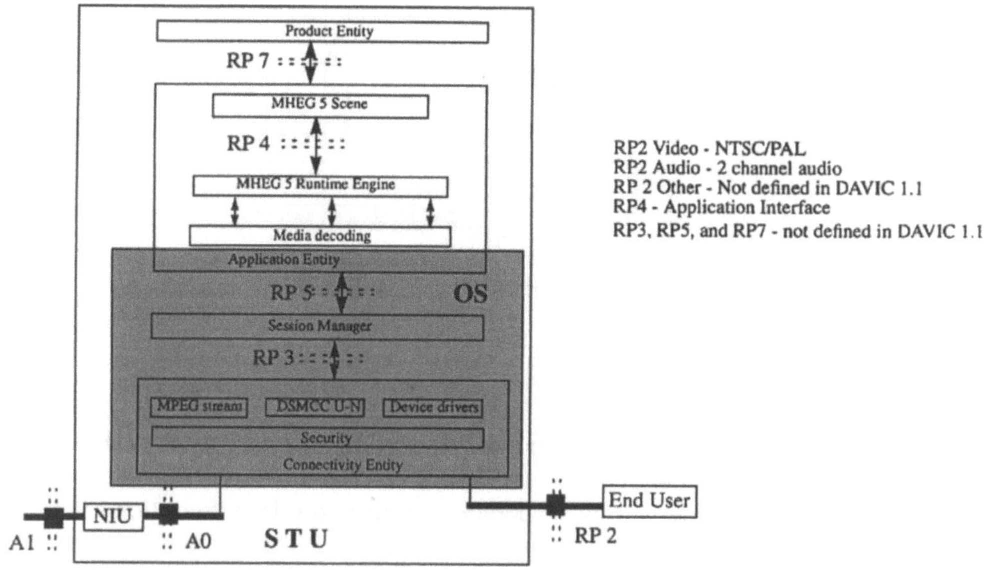

Figure 2. Common modules in an STU.

expected to include an in-house network and the ability to connect various peripherals in future extensions of the specification. SCS is connected to the Service Provider System (SPS) by means of a Delivery System (DS). Several interfaces were specified within a SCS, but only a few of them are defined in DAVIC 1.0. The STU should be able to decode MPEG-2 transport streams with one or more programs. The transport stream packets are mapped to ATM cells as specified by the ATM Forum with the restriction that two transport packet be mapped to eight ATM cells. The upper limit on the MPEG-2 video bitrate is 15 Mbps (Main Profile at Main Level). For compressed audio MPEG-1 audio is specified and MHEG 5 is specified for encoding multimedia objects. DAVIC does not specify how a SCS (STU) should be implemented. Only reference points in a SCS are specified and a compliant system should meet these specifications. Figure 2 shows the modules commonly found in the STUs and the interfaces specified by DAVIC between the modules.

In response to the growing popularity of Internet-based services, the extension DAVIC 1.1 includes additional tools in an STU to provide Internet services to the consumer. A Java virtual machine is used to provide Internet services. An external data port to the STU to connect a PC is also specified. In DAVIC 1.1 this is an Ethernet port. The Reference Decoder Model (RDM) is also specified to enable application developers to develop applications that execute on STUs. Figure 3 shows the RDM specified in DAVIC 1.1. This model is an extension of the MPEG-2 Transport System Target Decoder model (T-STD). Only the DAVIC extensions to the T-STD are shown in the figure. The data enters the transport buffer (TBn) from an MPEG-2 TS. The raw content used by the application is transferred to the content buffer (Bcontents) at a rate Rx(n) specified by the application. The coded MHEG 5 objects are transferred to a code buffer (Bcode). Bcode also contains the Java VM bytecode.

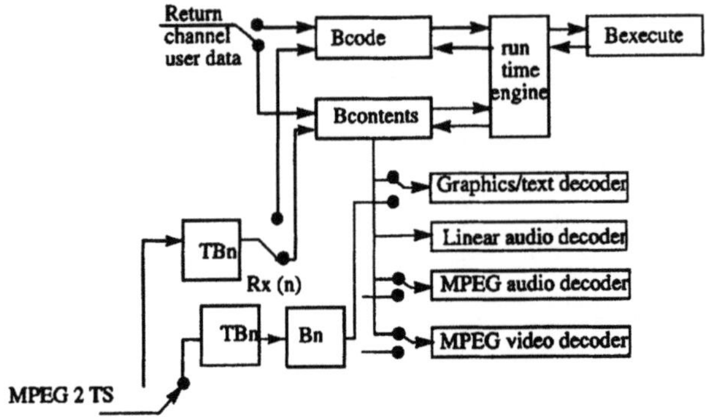

Figure 3. DAVIC reference decoder model.

The run-time engine executes the code in Bcode by loading it in to the memory (Bexecute) and controls the times at which contents are decoded and removed from Bcontents. Every DAVIC application includes a resource descriptor which provides information about the memory requirements, resolution and number of colors, and the transfer rate Rx(n), the rate of transfer from TBn to Bcontents and Bcode. Every DAVIC 1.1 compliant STU shall have a minimum buffer size of 128 KB for Bcode, 512 KB for Bcontents, and 128 KB for Bexecute.

1.2. Delivery system

Delivery System is a means to deliver information from a service provider to the service consumer. The means can be networked or non-networked (CD-ROM, tape etc.). In DAVIC 1.0 and 1.1 only networked delivery systems are considered. As shown in figure 1, the service provider and service consumer are connected by a delivery system and so are content provider and service provider. However, in DAVIC 1.0/1.1, only the delivery system between A9 and A1 reference points is considered.

The delivery system is composed of a core network and an access network. The core network is ATM based and for the access network several access types are supported. There is a defined reference point, A4, between the core network and the access network. For Hertzian access networks (satellite/terrestrial broadcast), the return channel over PSTN/ISDN networks to support interactivity is specified in the 1.1 extension.

DAVIC has responded to the growing popularity of the Internet by specifying tools for accessing Internet-based services using the STU. The tools specified in the 1.1 extension to achieve this are, STU data port to connect a PC to the STU, cable modem, and Java virtual machine. DAVIC Internet access provides the end user with 'full' or 'client' Internet access using a PC connected to the STU. The different levels of Internet access are defined in [3]. Figure 4 shows the protocol stack for Internet access with upstream traffic for all cases and for end-to-end ATM downstream traffic. Figure 5(a) shows the protocol stack used for down stream IP traffic when ATM terminates in the access network. In this case, IP packets are encapsulated in MPEG 2 transport stream packets. For IP over ATM, classical IP over ATM AAL 5 as specified in RFC 1483 and 1577 is used.

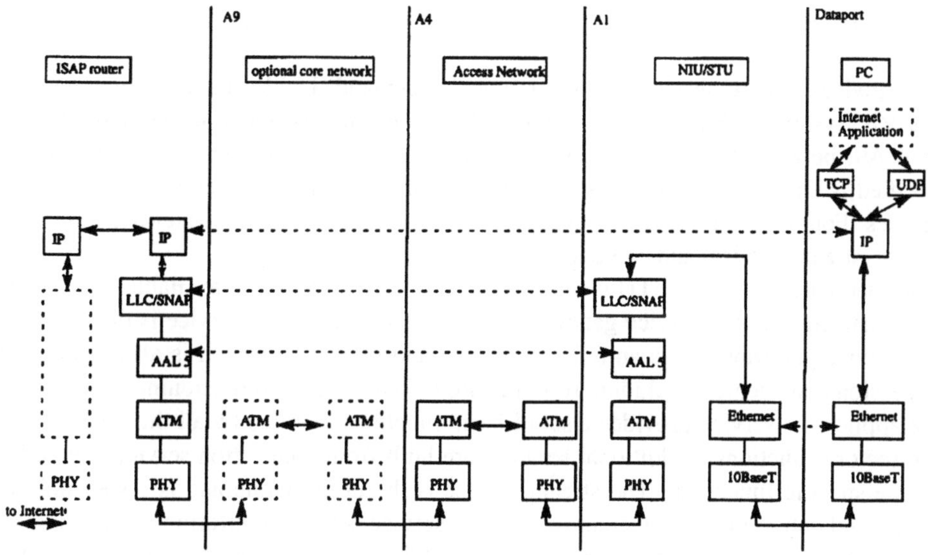

Figure 4. Internet access: upstream—all cases; downstream—ATM end-to-end.

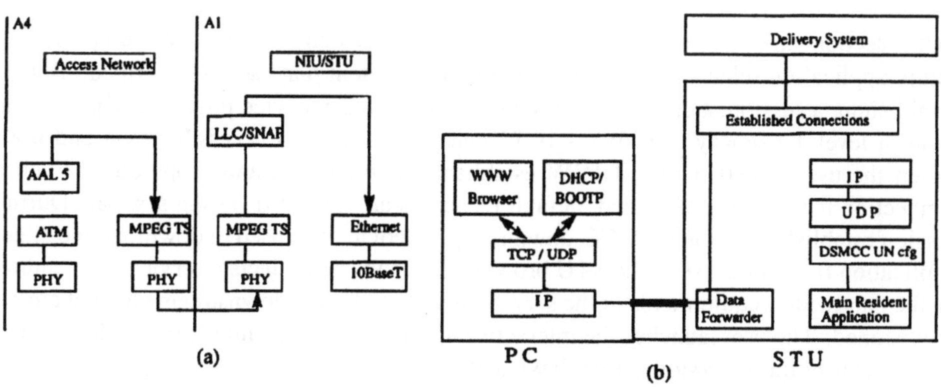

Figure 5. Internet access.

For Internet access, Internet Access Service Provider (ISAP) is pre-agreed between the network provider and the end user. A PC is connected to the STU dataport as shown in figure 5(b). In DAVIC 1.1 support of Ethernet on the PC-STU connection is normative [10]. Connection to the ISAP may be a pre-established through ATM PVCs or dynamically established using Q.2931 signaling. IP addresses may be pre-assigned or dynamically obtained using protocols such as DHCP. STU contains a data forwarder module which forwards the IP packets from the dataport (PC) to the network element. This module is responsible for LLC/SNAP encapsulation to and from the ISAP.

1.3. Service provider system

SPS provides DAVIC services such as movies on demand. Unlike the SCS components in a DAVIC system, SPS does not have internal reference points. Only an external reference point A9, between SPS and the core network, is specified. The server reference model specified is an object oriented distributed server model with a collection of well defined services. Four core services are specified in the server model: service gateway, application service, stream service, and content service.

Service gateway is the STU's entry point in a server. Services available from a SPS are registered with the service gateway and de-registered when a service is discontinued. The service gateway allows an STU to browse and select service. It is also responsible for session management including resource provisioning and re-provisioning for a session. The application service provides a set of basic functions required by all the services such as directory functions. Additional services are built from application services by adding service-specific functions. The stream service is the primary one and is responsible for storing and delivering media streams. Content service is used by information providers to install new services and content on the server. Additional services such as session gateway, file, client profile, and download service are also specified.

2. An end-to-end scenario in a DAVIC system

In this section, an end-to-end scenario including server selection, connection setup, session setup, application selection, content selection, and content playback is described. Before establishing a session, a client must first be able to locate a service provider. This is done using a level 1 gateway (L1GW). L1GW makes all the SPSs accessible to a end user. When the user selects a SPS, L1GW establishes a connection and drops out. When a connection is initially established, default resources are allocated for the session. During session establishment, the DSMCC-download protocol may be used to download the client application from the server. The STU browses the server and selects a service. Depending on the bandwidth requirements of the service, resources for the downstream channel are re-provisioned. The user launches the interactive application (e.g., a movie or a video game). When the user quits, session is tore down and resources are released.

3. DAVIC interoperability

To achieve its goal of global deployment of DAVIC systems and services, DAVIC places special emphasis on the interoperability of the sub-systems. Interoperability promotes global competition and speeds up the deployment of services to consumers. Since the DAVIC specification is made up of a number of independently developed standards, it is important to ensure that these standards work when used together in a DAVIC system. The work related to verifying the specification and its interoperability is undertaken by the Interoperability sub-group of DAVIC. The charter of the Interoperability sub-group is to verify that the specification does not have any 'gaps' and to provide guidelines for conformance testing. To promote the Interoperability efforts, DAVIC is promoting a series of interoperability events, the first of which took place at Columbia University in New York in June 1996 [2].

The New York *Interoperability Event* was held in parallel with the 13th DAVIC meeting in New York, hosted by the Image Technology for New Media Center (ITNM) [4] at Columbia University. It was the first multi-national DAVIC interoperability event organized and had the goal of testing and verifying the interfaces and protocols specified in DAVIC 1.0. A total of eight organizations from around the world participated in the event, interconnecting components (video servers, set-top-boxes, and applications) of different DAVIC-compliant video on demand systems with each other, using Columbia University's ATM network. The participating organizations were: Columbia University(USA), CSELT (Italy), DeTeBerkom/GMD FOKUS (Germany), GCL (Japan), GTE Labs (USA), Hewlett Packard IDACOM (Canada), NIST (USA) and NTT (Japan).

3.1. Interoperability configuration

The Interoperability demonstrations were shown for three days, June 18 and June 21 during the DAVIC meeting and on June 24 during the *Video on Demand Workshop*[1] [11] sponsored by the ITNM center. Over 350 people attended these demonstrations. The Interoperability testing took place in three phases during May–August 1996. Extensive testing was also done in addition to these demos.

Figure 6 shows the configuration used in the Interoperability experiments. All the participants except GTE setup their VOD systems in the labs of the ITNM center. GTE was connected to the ITNM center via a wide area ATM network. As shown in the figure, each participating organization had a client and a server connected to Columbia's ATM network. DeTeBerkom participated with a client. HP participated with test equipment which was used for measuring MPEG-2 transport stream parameters.

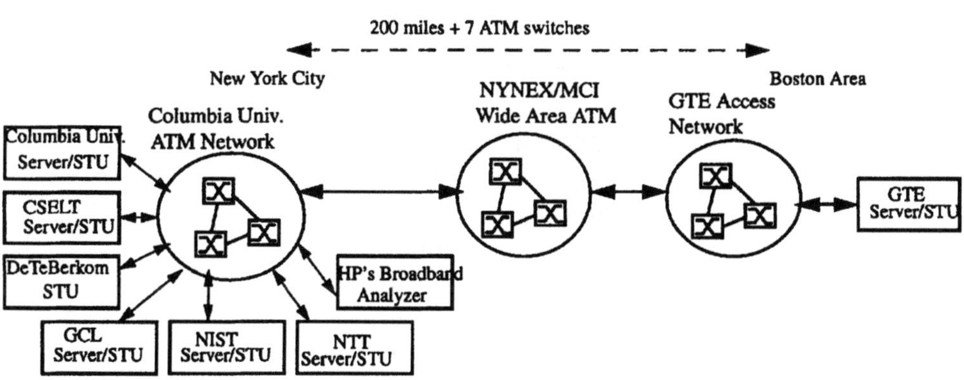

Figure 6. Interoperability test configuration.

The subnet of Columbia's ATM network used for the experiments was composed of three ATM switches: a FORE ASX100, a FORE ASX200, and an NEC Model-5 switch. The physical connections used multi-mode fiber and co-axial cable. The wide area connection included a DS3 link provided by NYNEX and MCI. It also included two ATM switches in the MCI segment and two ATM switches in the GTE local network.

The main emphasis of the experiments was to test S1 and S2 information flows at the A1 and A9 reference points as specified by DAVIC (see figure 1). A1 is the reference point between a SCS and the network while A9 is the reference point between the SPS and the network. The information flows are explained in Section 1. There are several reasons for restricting the scope of the Interoperability experiments to S1 and S2 information flows. At the time the experiments were conducted, there were no fully compliant DAVIC systems available. As a DAVIC system is very complex, it takes significant time and effort to build a complete system and there was not enough time before the event to build a complete system. The systems that were demonstrated were research prototypes. In the development of these prototypes, efforts were prioritized according to the importance of the information flows and S1, the MPEG data flow, and S2, the user control of the S1 flow, were developed first. This approach of prioritizing the information flows tested was also reflected in the decision of the Interoperability sub-group to develop conformance guidelines for S1 and S2 flows first.

The protocols specified by DAVIC for S1 and S2 information flows at A1 and A9 reference points are listed in columns 1 and 2 of Table 2. For the unidirectional S1 information flow from a server to a client, DAVIC specified MPEG-2(1) video and MPEG 1 audio. The MPEG data is packetized as packetized elementary streams (PES) and the PES packets are multiplexed into a MPEG 2 transport stream (TS) as specified in the MPEG 2 systems standard [6]. The transport stream packets are mapped to ATM AAL 5 PDUs with 2 TS packets mapped to 8 ATM cells. The physical layer specified by DAVIC is SONET. For the S2 bidirectional user control, DSMCC UU primitives are used [7]. The primitives are encoded using OMG's Common Data Representation (CDR) and the RPC used to invoke the control commands is OMG's UNO. For the transport layer TCP is specified. The IP packets are mapped to ATM using classical IP over ATM as specified in RFC 1577.

Table 2. Information flows at A1 and A9.

S1 flow	S2 flow
MPEG data	DSM-CC UU
PES	OMG-CDR
MPEG-2 TS	OMG-UNO
AAL 5	TCP
ATM	IP
SONET	AAL 5
—	ATM
—	SONET

All the systems were fully DAVIC compliant for S1 flow at A1 and A9 interfaces, i.e., protocols as specified by DAVIC for S1 information flow were implemented by all the systems. At the physical layer, DAVIC specifies SONET, while some participants used TAXI. This does not create problems as the ATM switch converts between the formats. For the S2 flow, NTT and GCL are fully DAVIC compliant. All other participants are DAVIC-compliant except in the RPC used (XDR/ORBIX is used instead of CDR/OMG UNO). As expected this caused interoperability problems the details of which are given in Section 3.3.

In the following tables, the first column contains the DAVIC tools for that information flow. In the cells corresponding to each organization, a YES indicates DAVIC compliance and in case where non-compliant, the alternative tool used is indicated.

3.2. *S1 interoperability*

S1 interoperability is the ability of a system to decode and display the S1 information delivered by another system. S1 interoperability was tested among all the participants except DeTeBerkom. DeTeBerkom took part only in S2 interoperability testing with CSELT. Since connection and session signaling was not used, to connect company A's server to company B's client, a PVC was established between these components. Also, since there was limited S2 interoperability among the participants (see Section 3.3 below), an MPEG-2 transport stream (TS) was delivered to the specific PVC without going through content selection by the client. Thus to test S1 interoperability between server A and client B, the server A delivers the stream to PVC *ab* and client B decodes the stream arriving on PVC *ab*. The S1 Interoperability testing verified the interoperability of MPEG-2 TS generated by individual organizations. For the purpose of these experiments, Columbia generated several TSs each with different encoding parameters such as PCR (program clock reference) frequency and PSI (program specific information) table frequency. Even though all these streams are compliant to the MPEG-2 systems standard, some of them were not decoded well by few decoders. The reason for this is different interpretation and use of these values by the decoders. NTT also tested the bitmaps and graphics delivery as specified by DAVIC. CSELT's and GCL's clients were able to decode both NTSC and PAL streams. Since the CSELT server had MPEG-2 video sequences encoded from PAL source, there were some problems in interoperating with it. DAVIC specifies that when an STU receives a 525/29.97 (625/25) encoded signal it produce a 525/29.97 (625/25) output at the RP2 video interface (see figure 2) [9]. This limits the usage of encoded content to the regions in which the source format is used. Further more, a global content producer is forced to maintain a copy of encoded stream for each TV standard. To overcome this STUs should be able to produce the output suitable for the local display system (TV) irrespective of the source format.

3.3. *S2 interoperability*

S2 information flow is a bidirectional flow used to transmit user control messages. If two systems have interoperable S2 flows, they can access each other's server and invoke DSMCC UU primitives to select and play video streams. S2 interoperability was tested between

CSELT—DeTeBerkom, CSELT—Columbia, Columbia—NIST, and Columbia—GTE. This was possible as these companies have implemented the draft international standard (DIS) version of the DSMCC UU specification and use the same protocol stack for the S2 flow. For S2 interoperability testing between CSELT and DeTeBerkom, the test scenario consisted of DeTeBerkom's client retrieving MHEG5 objects from CSELT server and decoding the MHEG5 objects and controlling the streams using the DSM-CC primitives. In the S2 testing done between Columbia's client and CSELT server, file and stream objects (MPEG-2 TS) were accessed by Columbia's client from CSELT server. Columbia and NIST were able to demonstrate full S2 interoperability, including server access, content selection and MPEG-2 stream playback.

3.4. *Test methodology and results*

Testing was mainly based on observation. A broadband MPEG-2 analyzer from HP was also used to measure PCR interval and PCR jitter. To test S1 information flow, an MPEG-2 TS was delivered to a client and the quality of audio and video was observed. In case of problems, causes were explored. A cross-connection from company A's server to company B's client is considered working (interoperable) if video and audio were played back without any disruptions. The results of S1 and S2 flow interoperability among the participants are summarized in Table 3.

In Table 3, for a cell corresponding to A's server and B's client, the following conventions are used:

W	works without problems
w	works when pumping TS generated by B but problems encountered when TS generated by A was used
blank cell	scenario was not tested
m	works with minor problems
D	does not work

Table 3. S2 interoperability testing summary.

	Client													
Server	Columbia		CSELT		DeTeBerkom		GCL		GTE		NIST		NNT	
Information flow	S1	S2	S1	S2	S1	S2	S1	S2	S1	Ss2	S1	S2	S1	S2
Columbia	W	W	m	m			w		W	W	W	W	w	
CSELT	w	m	W	W		W	W						w	
GCL	W		W				W	W					W	
GTE	W								W	W				
NIST	W	W	m				w				W	W	w	
NTT	W		m				D						W	W

There were two reasons for untested scenarios (blank cells in the table). In the case involving GTE the reason was that the wide area ATM connection connecting GTE's server and client to Columbia University was not available during the first two phases when most of the testing was done. In the case involving NIST, the reason was that NIST's client had a software decoder which can decode bitrates of less than 1.5 Mbps and only Columbia's server had such low bitrate TS.

Since the systems tested were research prototypes, we cannot attribute the interoperability problems totally to 'gaps' in the DAVIC specification. Some of the problems faced could be due to implementation problems. The S1 interoperability problems between CSELT and other participants were due to the restriction in the DAVIC specification as explained in Section 3.2. In some cases the decoded video was jerky. This depends on the jitter tolerance of the client system. Since all the servers used were software based running on general purpose operating systems, the output of the server cannot be guaranteed to be constant bit rate. This results in packet jitter at the output of the server which could contribute to jerky video in some decoders depending on the decoder's jitter tolerance.

As shown in Table 3, the S2 flow was implemented by all organizations but interoperability could not be achieved among the majority of the participants. This is mainly because of the incompatible RPC mechanism used and the level of compliance to the DSMCC UU specification. It should be noted that the applications tested were simple, use a small percentage of the DSMCC UU primitives, and the servers are accessed by one user at a time for all the participating servers except Columbia's server which allows multiple user access. It is not clear how the RPC specified by DAVIC (OMG UNO) scales when the services are commercially deployed and accessed by thousands of users at the same time.

4. Conclusion

DAVIC is playing an important role in the global deployment of broadband audio-visual services. Currently DAVIC has successfully released its first specification 1.0 and also its first extension 1.1. Work is being continued to extend the specification to provide advanced services to consumers. Verifying the specification through interoperability experiments increases the credibility of the specification and encourages the industry to manufacture DAVIC compliant systems. The interoperability event provided an opportunity for all the participants to test and verify their implementation of the DAVIC specification. S1 flow interoperability was thoroughly tested while S2 flow interoperability was not completely tested. From these experiments, it can be concluded that the incompatibilities were mainly in content generation. There were some unsettled mismatches between some MPEG-2 transport streams and some decoders. This could be due to different interpretation and handling of timing information by the decoders. Continued interoperability testing is necessary to identify the problems in the DAVIC specifications. The second in a series of DAVIC interoperability events was held during the Tokyo Electronic Show in October 1996. This event also includes S3 flow interoperability in addition to S1 and S2 flows.

Acknowledgments

Acknowledgments are due to the other members of Columbia's VOD team [1] for their contributions to the testbed. Acknowledgments are also due to the organizations and their representatives (primary contact listed below) that took part in the event.

Organization	Contact Person	E-Mail
CSELT, Italy	Stefano Dal Lago	stefano.dallago@cselt.stet.it
DeTe Berkom, Germany	Hans Werner Bitzer	bitzer@deteberkom.de
GCL, Japan	Shigeru Komatsu	komat@gctech.co.jp
GTE Labs, USA	Len Ulbricht	lwu1@gte.com
HP IDACOM, Canada	Trevor Dyck	trevord@idacom.hp.com
NIST, USA	David Hsu	su@isdn.ncsl.nist.gov
NTT, Japan	Hisashi Kasahara	kasahara@nttvdt.hil.ntt.jp

Columbia University acknowledges C-Cube, GTE Labs, HP-IDACOM, IBM, NEC, NYNEX, and SGI for their support for the testbed infrastructure.

Note

1. For a copy of the proceedings, please send an e-mail to hari@itnm.columbia.edu.

References

1. S.-F. Chang, A. Eleftheriadis, D. Anastassiou, S. Jacobs, H. Kalva, and J. Zamora, "Columbia's VoD and multimedia research testbed with heterogeneous network support," appears in this special issue, Intern. J. on Multimedia Tools and Applications, Kluwer Academic Publishers, May 1997.
2. Columbia University, "DAVIC New York interoperability experiments: report and results," DAVIC Contribution No. DAVIC/TC/SYS/96/09/008, Geneva, Switzerland, 1996.
3. D. Crocker, "To be on the Internet," RFC 1775, IETF, March 1995.
4. DAVIC VoD Interoperability Test Event, June 1996, Columbia University, New York (http://www.itnm.columbia.edu/vod/interop96).
5. A. Eleftheriadis, "Architecting Video-on-Demand systems: DAVIC 1.0 and beyond," Proceedings, International Symposium on Multimedia Communications and Video Coding, Brooklyn, NY, Oct. 1995.
6. Generic Coding of Moving Pictures and Associated Audio (MPEG 2 Systems), ISO/IEC 13818-1, International Standard, 1995.
7. Generic Coding of Moving Pictures and Associated Audio (DSMCC), ISO/IEC 13818-6, International Standard, 1996.
8. The Digital Audio-Visual Council (DAVIC), "Part 2—systems reference models and scenarios," DAVIC 1.0 specification, Geneva, Switzerland, 1995.
9. The Digital Audio-Visual Council (DAVIC), "Part 5—service consumer system and high level API," DAVIC 1.0 specification, 1995.
10. The Digital Audio-Visual Council (DAVIC), "Internet access tools," Baseline document No. 28, DAVIC 1.1 specification, 1996.
11. VOD96, Workshop on Video on Demand: Technology, Interoperability, and Trials, URL: http://www.itnm.columbia.edu/workshopo/vod96.

Hari Kalva received the B.Tech. degree from N.B.K.R. Institute to Science and Technology, S.V. University, Tirupati, India in 1991 and the M.S. from Florida Atlantic University, Boca Raton, FL in 1994.

From Jan. 1995 to Aug. 1996, he was a Research Staff Associate in the ADVENT project at Columbia University. He is currently a Ph.D. student in the Department of Electrical Engineering at Columbia University. His research interests include Multimedia Communication Systems and protocols.

Shih-Fu Chang is currently an Associate Professor at Department of Electrical Engineering and Center for Telecommunications Research in Columbia University. He received the M.S. and Ph.D. degree in Electrical Engineering and Computer Science from the University of California at Berkeley in 1991 and 1993, respectively.

Dr. Chang's current research interests include content-based image technologies for multimedia systems, visual information systems, and image/video signal processing and communications. At Columbia, he is co-leading the development of a Video-on-Demand/Multimedia Testbed, and Columbia's audio-visual service interoperability experiments. His group has developed several advanced prototypes in visual information systems, including an image/video search and cataloging engine, WebSEEk, and a Web-based compressed video editing and search system, CVEPS.

He was the recipient of the best paper award of SPIE International Symposium on Visual Communications and Image Processing 1995, the best student paper award of the ACM first Multimedia Conference 1993, an NSF CAREER award 1995–8, and an IBM University Research Partnership (Faculty Development) Award 1995–7. He serves on the editorial boards and program committees of several international conferences and publications. He was the organizer and co-chair of Workshop on Video on Demand Systems—Technology, Interoperability and Trials, held at Columbia University in June 1996.

Alexandros Eleftheriadis was born in Athens, Greece, in 1967. He received the Diploma in Electrical Engineering and Computer Science from the National Technical University of Athens, Greece, in 1990, and the M.S., M.Phil., and Ph.D. degrees in Electrical Engineering from Columbia University, New York, in 1992, 1994, and 1995 respectively.

Since 1995 he has been an Assistant Professor in the Department of Electrical Engineering at Columbia University, where he is leading a research team working in the areas of video signal processing and compression, video communication systems, distributed multimedia systems, and the fundamentals of compression. During the summers of 1993 and 1994, he was with AT&T Bell Laboratories, Murray Hill, NJ, developing low bit rate video coding techniques for videoconferencing applications. From 1990 until 1995, he was a Graduate Research Assistant in the Department of Electrical Engineering at Columbia University.

Prof. Eleftheriadis is a member of the ANSI X3L3.1 Committee, and is participating in the ISO/IEC JTC1/SC29/WG11 (MPEG) standardization activity as well as DAVIC. He is also a member of the IEEE, the ACM, and the Technical Chamber of Greece.

Multimedia Tools and Applications 5, 133–146 (1997)

ARMIDA^{TM}: Multimedia Applications across ATM-Based Networks Accessed via Internet Navigation

STEFANO DAL LAGO, GUIDO FRANCESCHINI, PIETRO MARCHISIO, MARCO MESTURINO, ENRICO POLESE AND GIOVANNI VENUTI
CSELT—Centro Studi E Laboratori Telecomunicazioni via G. Reiss Romoli, 274-10148, Turin, Italy

Abstract. ARMIDA^{TM} (Applications **R**etrieving **M**ultimedia **I**nformation **D**istributed over **A**TM) is a prototypical system for experimental applications based on the interactive retrieval of multimedia information from remote data bases over ATM networks. ARMIDA^{TM} aims at being compliant with the specifications issued by the "Digital Audio Visual Council" (DAVIC) for interactive multimedia services and applications, as well as at representing a sample implementation of the system specified in DAVIC 1.0. The present paper illustrates the way ARMIDA^{TM} works to provide these applications, by describing the system hardware and software architecture and its main components, with a particular concern towards the way they interact to implement the required functionality.

Keywords: multimedia, ATM, DAVIC, internet

1. Introduction

ARMIDA^{TM} (Applications **R**etrieving **M**ultimedia **I**nformation **D**istributed over **A**TM) is a prototypical system for experimental applications based on the interactive retrieval of multimedia information from remote data bases over ATM networks.

ARMIDA^{TM} aims at being compliant with the specifications issued by the "Digital Audio Visual Council" (DAVIC) for interactive multimedia services and applications, as well as at representing a sample implementation of the system specified in DAVIC 1.0. The main objectives of the ARMIDA^{TM} project within CSELT are to collect and integrate the wide range of expertise involved in the design of such a complex system in order to validate DAVIC specifications and to provide a reference implementation for future DAVIC conformance testing tools.

The end user, operating a commercial PC (with MS-Windows NT) which acts as the system terminal, accesses a number of applications through a popular Internet browser, enjoying the multimedia contents by means of a user friendly graphical interface.

Currently, the "Movies On Demand" and "News On Demand" applications are available, all based on the same basic service paradigm. They are experimental arrangements, providing a subset, though significant, of the full range of functionality which are likely to be offered by the corresponding commercial applications.

Increasingly enhanced versions of the ARMIDA^{TM} system have been demonstrated during a number of events since June '95. In June '96 ARMIDA^{TM} also participated in the first DAVIC interoperability event in New York.

Since ARMIDA™ targets the compliance with the specifications issued by DAVIC 1.0 [3], terms adopted by DAVIC will often be inserted (*in italics*) in the following to indicate components or entire subsystems; moreover, the correspondence between the main building blocks of ARMIDA™ and the relevant entities within the DAVIC *System Reference Model* will be highlighted.

Neither the details of the internal structure, nor the functioning of each component (device or program module) are given in the following, whereas reference to the appropriate standards (where public domain technologies are used) or to specific publications is made.

2. System architecture

The ARMIDA™ hardware architecture is depicted in figure 1(a). Three types of entities can be seen in it: terminals, network links and servers.

Within the terminal, or *Set-Top Box* (*STB*), two functionally distinct parts can be isolated. The former, called *Set-Top Unit* (*STU*), performs the processing needed to manage the interaction with the end user and to implement his commands (data requests, information receipt and presentation, sending of messages); the latter, named *Network Interface Unit* (*NIU*), provides the connection to the network. The two modules communicate through an interface, indicated as A0, which is specified by DAVIC.

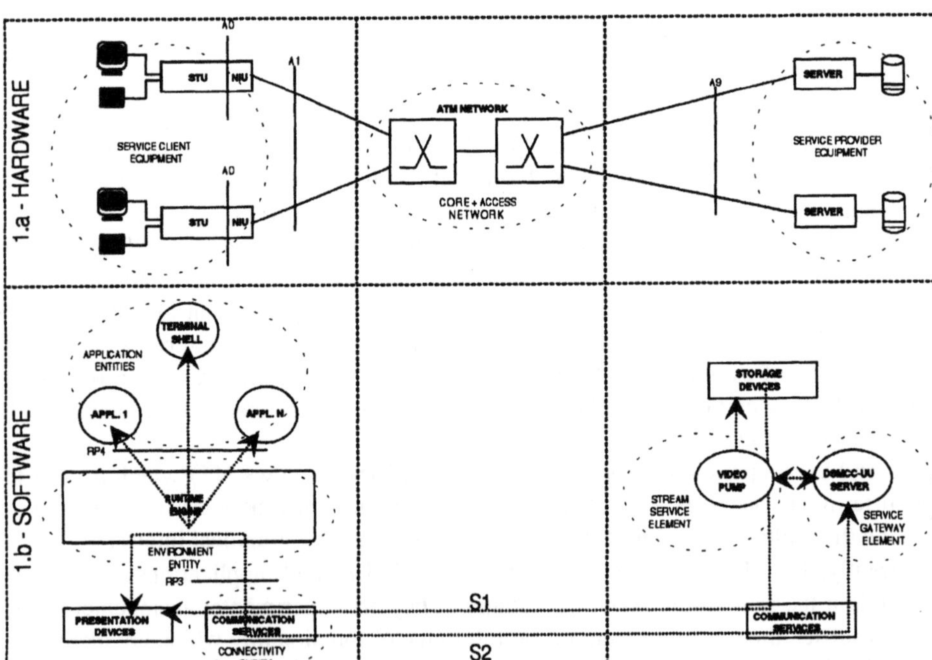

Figure 1. ARMIDA™ hardware (a) and software, (b) overall architecture.

The *NIU* is connected (A1 reference point) to a Fore System ASX200 ATM switch which is actually part of a Corporate Local ATM LAN: a few options for the physical layer have been implemented so far (25 Mbit/s on Cat. 3, 4 or 5 unshielded twisted pairs and 100 Mbit/s TAXI on multi-mode optical fiber). At the moment ATM Forum signaling UNI3.0 is used to set-up connections, as that is the only signalling protocol currently supported by the Fore System switch. The servers feed the terminals through the ATM network with the requested multimedia material which they retrieve from dedicated mass-storage devices (disk arrays up to about 100 GBytes). The servers are connected (A9 reference point), via 100 Mbit/s TAXI or 155 Mbit/s SDH multi-mode optical links, to the CSELT Corporate ATM network as well. Once again, UNI3.0 signaling is available at the server to manage both IP and non-IP connections. The connection of the Corporate ATM LAN to the Italian and European ATM Networks easily allows to run the system (using however PVCs instead of SVCs) in WAN trans-national configurations, as it has been the case for a number of demonstration events.

The hardware architecture depicted above matches a distribution of the software modules inside the system as indicated in figure 1(b). The S1 flow (marked with a bold dotted line in the figure), is comprised of the so-called *Content Information*, i.e., in this particular case, of the MPEG coded sequences which the terminal retrieves and presents upon user request. The S2 flow (represented with a light dotted line in the figure), contains the *Control Information*, i.e., the messages which the terminal sends to the server to request multimedia contents, as well as the data (MHEG-5 objects, text, still images) that the client expects in response. Of course, the S1 flow is uni-directional, whilst the S2 flow is bi-directional.

It is worthwhile to remark that the hardware and software structure described above are substantially compliant with the *System Reference Model* produced by DAVIC 1.0. To stress that, the element of the DAVIC 1.0 reference model which has a functional correspondence with each part of ARMIDA™ is marked with a dotted line in figures 1(a) and 1(b).

In the following the *Set-Top Box* and server components of the system will be examined in more detail, considering in particular the way S1 and S2 flows are handled.

3. Client architecture

3.1. Hardware architecture

The ARMIDA™ *STB* is based on a standard IBM-compatible PC platform with ISA/PCI bus architecture and running MS-Windows NT. From the hardware viewpoint four sections can be identified in figure 2(a) from the top to the bottom:

- The PC motherboard, controlling local mass storage and input peripherals like keyboard and mouse (optionally replaceable by an infrared remote control); it also supervises data transfer over the two buses.
- An ATM NIU card developed by CSELT, handling the interfaces A1 (towards the network) and A0 (towards the MPEG decoding hardware of the STU).
- A full (Audio, Video and System) MPEG decoding board developed by CSELT (M-BIRD), which feeds the PC motherboard with S2 data and the overlay board with decoded S1 data (audio and video).

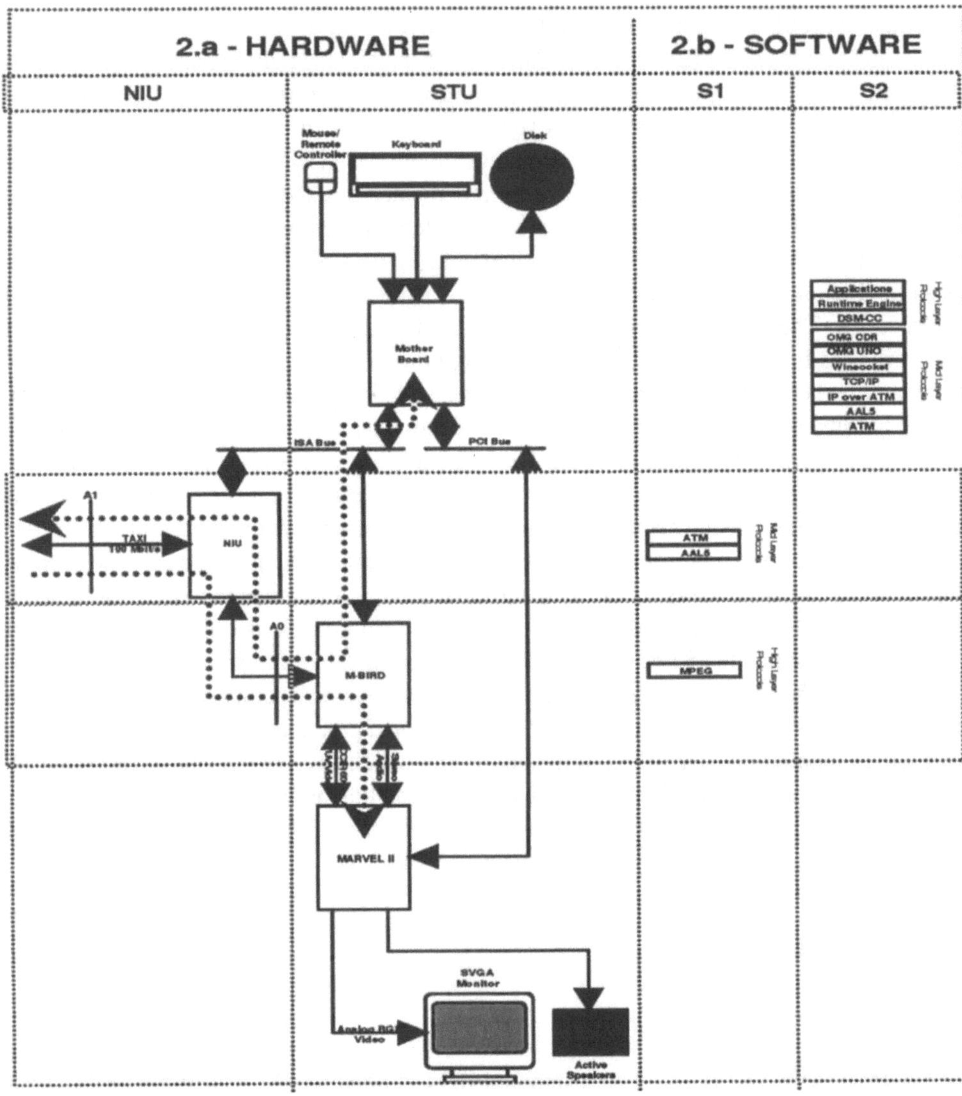

Figure 2. ARMIDA™ *STB* hardware (a) and software (b) architecture.

- A commercial overlay board (currently MARVEL II from Matrox) which mixes SVGA graphics with decoded MPEG video and processes the analogue audio produced by the MPEG decoder, allowing the user to change various parameters (volume, balance, ...) of the audio presentation.

Figure 2(b) depicts, for S1 and S2 flows, the organization of communication software in the *STU* and the way it is allocated to the four hardware sections listed above.

The ATM and AAL5 protocols are executed in the *NIU* for the S1 flow, whereas the *NIU* and the decoding board acts just as a pass-through for S2 ATM cells, which are handled in software by the PC together with the higher layer software. Similarly, ATM cells carrying signaling information (S4 flow) are also completely handled in software.

3.2. Software architecture

On the terminal, at the highest logical level the applications are based upon ISO/MHEG (Multimedia and Hypermedia Experts Group) "objects" containing the coded information ("actions" and data structures) to manage the interaction with the end user, in particular for navigation among multimedia contents, and the real-time events associated with the fruition of the material itself (e.g., VCR-like commands: Play, Stop, Pause, Slow Motion, Fast Forward, Fast Reverse, Random Access).

The application objects are interpreted by the *Runtime Engine* program. The ISO/MHEG-5 standard [8] defines the way these commands are included and coded inside the applications. Such standard specifies the interaction between a layer of interpreted software (the applications), which potentially is machine independent, and a layer of compiled software (the *Runtime Engine*) which is specific for the hardware of the terminal. This interaction is identified by DAVIC 1.0 with the term *High Level* API and labeled RP4.

The Runtime Engine exploits a Communications Services API, which is in charge of the transport of the S1 and S2 flows between the server and the terminal; the relevant DAVIC 1.0 reference point is named RP3 (or Communications API). The coded material received at the terminal (except for the MPEG streams, that are directly sent to the decoding hardware) goes to the Runtime Engine which sends it to the relevant presentation units. The set of functions that decode and display multimedia contents is grouped under the generic label Presentation Devices in the figure.

The protocol stacks defined by DAVIC 1.0 for the S1 and S2 flows in ATM networks are depicted in figures 3 and 4. The specific pieces of software by means of which the various S2 layers are implemented in the ARMIDA™ *STB* as well as the relevant programming interfaces are also reported in the middle of figure 4. All of the S1 layers are implemented in hardware.

Figure 5 shows the S4 protocol stack as implemented within ARMIDA™. The ATM Signaling protocol is the ATM Forum spec. UNI 3.0: this is different from the ITU-T recommendation Q.2931 selected by DAVIC1.0 for the S4 flow, but it has been chosen for the ARMIDA™ system due to the fact that commercial ATM switches currently only widely support UNI 3.0. As soon as better support to Q.2931 will be available in the switching nodes, ARMIDA™ will also move to Q.2931.

MPEG-2 Transport Stream (Single Program TS)
AAL 5
ATM
Physical Layer

Figure 3. Protocol stack for S1 flow.

MHEG-5 based applications	Movies on Demand	News on Demand	
	MHEG-5 Engine		DSM-CC UU IDL
DSM-CC UU	DSM Library		
OMG-CDR	Orbix 2.0.2		
OMG-UNO			Windows Socket 1.1
TCP	WINSOCK.DLL		*Transport Driver Interface*
IP	MSTCP.DLL		*NDIS 3.x*
RFC 1577	CSNIU.SYS KERNEL DRIVER		
AAL5			
ATM			*ISA bus*
Physical Layer	100 Mbit/s TAXI or 25 Mbit/s on UTP		

Figure 4. Protocol stack for S2 flow and ARMIDA™ implementation.

UNI 3.0
SSCOP
AAL 5
ATM
Physical Layer

Figure 5. Protocol stack for S4 flow.

In the following a brief description of the key software developments of ARMIDA™ is provided.

3.2.1. MHEG-5 based applications. The terminal is capable to run a wide range of applications, e.g., "Movies On Demand" or "News on Demand"; these applications are based upon ISO/MHEG (Multimedia and Hypermedia Experts Group) "objects" and retrieve the various multimedia contents from the server using the ISO DSM-CC UU standard (Digital Storage Media Command and Control, User to User) [9]. Both MHEG-5 objects and data contents (e.g.: bitmaps and texts) are exchanged through the DSM-CC UU File interface, while the control of the video bitstream is performed through the DSM-CC UU Stream interface.

The multimedia applications the terminal is able to run are encoded in MHEG-5, the emerging joint ISO/ITU standard for the "coding of base level interactive applications". MHEG-5 has been designed to support the distribution of interactive multimedia applications in a client-server architecture across heterogeneous platforms, with the objective of ensuring interoperability across minimal resources platforms. That requires the capability to have an application residing on the server, with only the portions that at a given moment are needed for presentation downloaded to the client, which is responsible to have a *Run-Time Engine* (the MHEG-5 Engine) able to interpret the MHEG-5 objects making part of an application, to present them to the user and to manage local interaction with him.

Figure 6. Root scene of the "Movies On Demand" application.

The demonstrated applications are basic examples of interactive multimedia service. They supports user navigation in term of transitions between scenes. The available web is tree-like organized. The user begins with a root scene and proceeds towards the desired leaf scene by navigating through a path of intermediate scenes. When he gets the desired leaf scene, he is able to control the playback of the referred MPEG sequence via a set of VCR-like buttons. As an example, the root scene of the "Movies on Demand" application is reproduced in figure 6.

All demonstrated applications have been generated by means of *MediaTouch*™, a visual based authoring tool (under development at CSELT) specifically devoted to create/modify MHEG-5 objects.

3.2.2. DSM-CC User-User. The DSM-CC UU core interfaces have been almost completely implemented in ARMIDA™ and form a library which is then linked by the MHEG-5 Engine. Available interfaces include:

- Directory: to manage the bindings between logical names and physical data.
- Stream: to control the real-time delivery of the MPEG streams (e.g., VCR commands).
- File: to provide random access (read/write) to ordinary (no streams) files.

3.2.3. ATM related protocols. The major effort in the implementation of the DAVIC mid layers protocols for S2 flow has been the integration of the ATM *NIU* developed by CSELT within the standard Microsoft networking environment. Namely, running the TCP/IP stack over a special network adapter has called for the development of a custom Network Device Driver compliant with NDIS (Network Device Interface Specification): in particular NDIS 3.1 defines a 32 bit kernel mode driver, binary compatible between Windows NT and '95.

The kernel driver written for the ATM *NIU* internally implements the Request For Comment 1577 "Classical IP over ATM" [10] with AAL5 encapsulation [7] specifications. The kernel driver is also responsible for the AAL5 and ATM layers, which are executed by the host CPU exchanging ATM cells with the *NIU* through the ISA bus.

4. Server architecture

4.1. Hardware architecture

The ARMIDA^{TM} main server is based on a commercial UNIX multiprocessor system (SUN SS1000) equipped with about 80 GBytes of mass storage (disk array technology with FiberChannel interface), 128 MBytes RAM and four 85 MHz CPUs. An ATM board (FORE SBA200 or SUNATM2) with 155 Mbit/s SDH multimode optical interface has been added to provide ATM connectivity. Other smaller servers (SUN SS20 workstations with 4 to 16 GBytes of mass storage, 32 MBytes RAM, a single 60 MHz CPU and ATM board) are used for development and on-the-road demonstration purposes. All the servers run the SUN Solaris 2.5 operating system and benefit in particular of the real time scheduler and multithread support offered by this environment. It is worthwhile to remark that it was decided to use a general purpose platform because commercial availability, fast software development and scalability aspects have been privileged with respect to pure performance parameters.

Compliance with the physical layers specified by DAVIC 1.0 at the A9 interface is achieved at the 34 Mbit/s PDH UNI of the Corporate ATM LAN with the public network.

As far as performances and traffic shaping are concerned, a general problem exists in the granularity of the bandwidth physically allocatable, which is not 1 bit/s. The FORE SBA200 board only allows to space one flow at a time, thus preventing concurrent delivery of MPEG-2 bitstreams. Moreover, the granularity of the spacer is not well documented and only empirical values have been selected which are able to satisfy the network and decoder buffer requirements for specific bitrates. Instead, the SUNATM2 board allows for both tight bandwidth control (the granularity is 64 Kbit/s and it has been verified through the monitoring of the traffic generated) and concurrent spacing—even at different bitrates—of several channels.

Initial tests conducted with the SUNATM2 board have shown the ability of the ARMIDA^{TM} main server to sustain the delivery of up to 7 different bitstreams at 6 Mbit/s when using the default MPEG-2 over ATM mapping (that is 2 MPEG-2 Transport Packets per AAL5-PDU; it causes about 2000 send-operations per second per stream). Different mappings, using longer AAL5-PDUs and thus less send-operations per second, have been proven to augment the performances, sustaining up to about 15 different bitstreams at 6 Mbit/s when using 38 MPEG-2 Transport Packets per AAL5-PDU.

Lower performances have been obtained using the smaller ARMIDA^{TM} server configuration, able to deliver up to about 16 Mbit/s of aggregate bandwidth when using the default MPEG-2 over ATM mapping. More extensive tests and performance measurements are underway.

4.2. Software architecture

A DSMCC-UU Server program terminates the S2 Flow protocol stack. It implements the DSM-CC User-to-User Core Consumer Interfaces and is in charge of managing the access to the offered services from the ARMIDA^{TM} terminals. It handles databases for applications (MHEG-5 objects), simple contents (text, bitmaps ...) and MPEG streams.

Every time an ARMIDA^{TM} terminal connects to the ARMIDA^{TM} server, it is actually connected to the DSMCC-UU Server program. When the client requests a bitstream then the DSMCC-UU Server launches (and then controls) another process (the Video Pump). Optimizations are in progress to better exploit the multi-threading techniques and avoid spawning separate processes.

A Video Pump program is responsible for the setup of the S1 connection (see chapter 7) and for the real time delivery of the MPEG bitstream and its control.

To enable the Fast modes in the delivery of MPEG Streams, a shadow file is off-line computed which contains a number of indexes and other useful information (instantaneous bitrate, to possibly evolve towards Variable Bit Rate support, Presentation Time Stamps ...). This allows the prompt individuation of Intra coded images, which are actually delivered, while Predictive and Bi-interpolated pictures are skipped.

4.3. Multimedia contents

The database at the server comprises both audio-visual bitstreams and other contents: in particular MHEG-5 objects, bitmaps and text files. As far as the audio-visual information is concerned, both MPEG-1 and MPEG-2 coded material is used; however, in all cases, the elementary audio and video streams are multiplexed into an MPEG-2 Single Program Transport Stream. As a result, they appear from a network perspective just as MPEG-2 Transport Streams coded at different bitrates (usually 8 or 6 Mbit/s for the MPEG-2 sequences, and about 1.5 Mbit/s for the MPEG-1 material).

5. Internet access

Two different approaches have been considered to address the issue of navigating among multimedia information and selecting a certain service to actually view the chosen content.

The so-called all-DAVIC solution, depicted in figure 7(a), consists in adopting the full DAVIC 1.0 protocol structure and to base upon it all of the implemented services, including the Navigation application. This essentially implies that navigation sessions between the terminal and the selected servers are established by means of the DSM-CC UN (User-to-Network) [9] protocol while DSM-CC UU is used to navigate within a server. The Navigation application is then a set of MHEG-5 objects and the information it retrieves from a server should be in the form of MHEG-5 objects too.

In the alternative approach, illustrated in figure 7(b), the Navigation application relies upon the HTTP (Hyper-Text Transfer Protocol) protocol, an industry standard in the Internet world for which thousands of server sites are already existing. The navigation application has just to handle hypertext files in the HTML (Hyper-Text Markup Language) format like many commercial World Wide Web products already do.

As soon as the terminal, by using the above mechanisms, has found the final address of the piece of content the user wants to access, it can switch to the DAVIC protocol stacks in

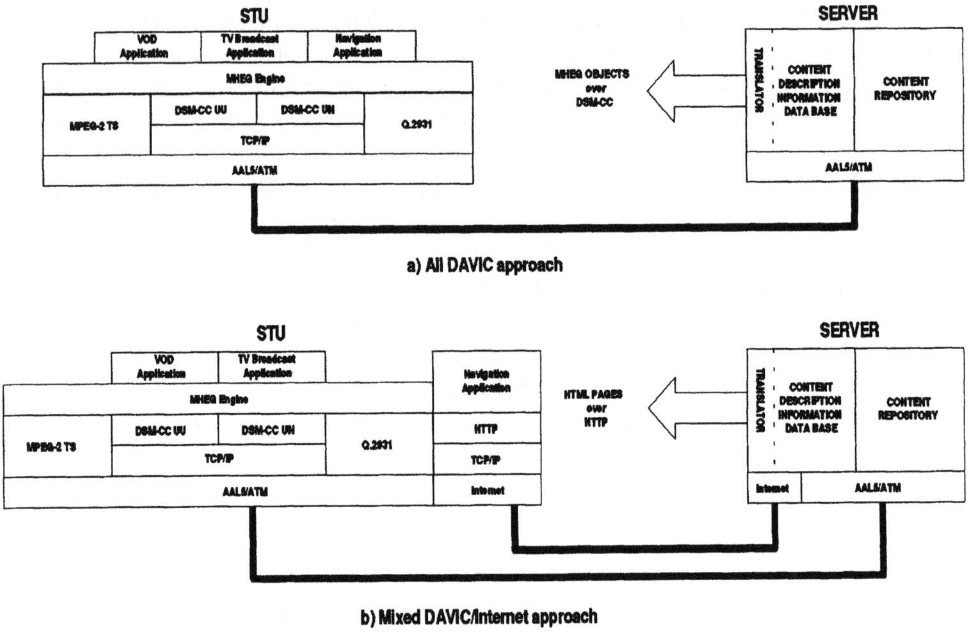

Figure 7. Two approaches for the navigation application.

order to open an application session, to download the content-specific application code in the form of MHEG-5 objects and to control the content retrieval in the usual DAVIC style. The address information stored on the server has of course to include all the items needed by the DSM-CC UN and UU to initiate the application session.

It has to be noted that within this approach, which mixes together elements from the DAVIC and the Internet worlds, there is a common bulk of software represented by the TCP/IP protocol stack.

The ARMIDA™ applications are accessible through this second approach: the user operates the terminal using a commercial Internet browser (Netscape 3.0) and a Helper Application. The selection of a URL (Uniform Resource Locator) containing a file with extension ".dsm" automatically triggers the DAVIC engine (an MHEG-5 engine enhanced with DSM-CC UU available in the local environment as the Helper Application). The .dsm file contains the information needed to locate the server and the MHEG-5 root object inside that server. The information contained in the .dsm file is passed by the browser to the DAVIC engine, which uses the address to setup a connection through ATM signaling for the S2 flow (see chapter 7), downloads the MHEG-5 root object and enters the MHEG-5 based application provided by the selected service.

This method to provide clients with service providers addresses is fair in nature, easy to use (Internet and Internet browsing tools are already widespread and well known by a significant portion of the potential users of Video Retrieval services) and easy to maintain. The number and nature of the parameters in the .dsm file are subject to further analysis. Moreover, the possibility of using Plug-ins instead of Helper applications is under study.

By the way, DAVIC/Internet integration approaches similar to the one described above are being considered for DAVIC 1.2 specification, due by the end of 1996.

6. Ongoing activities

The present paper has described the status of the ARMIDA™ system as it is today. A number of activities are still ongoing or planned, in the direction of both increasing the system functionality and extending the coverage of DAVIC 1.0 aspects. The main issues at stake are:

- Development of new interactive applications (e.g., games).
- Implementation of selected DSM-CC UU Extended Interfaces (e.g.: download, security) and linkage with database services (to provide a more complete server environment and integrate expertise which is important in a real server architecture).
- Introduction of DSM-CC UN protocol for session control (S3 flow): this is an integral part of the DAVIC 1.0 system architecture.
- Extension of DAVIC1.0 tools for the transport of the S1 flow over IP.
- Level 1 Gateway functionality in the network: this item is somehow related to the previous one. Intelligent Network architectures are being considered to provide a wider range of services and other ways to access services.
- Usage of other "standard" access networks (HFC, FTTC/FTTB, wireless): this would provide additional value to the ARMIDA™ system, allowing for a wider range of applicability of both the concepts and the reference implementation.
- Support within ARMIDA™ clients of the ETSI/EBU DVB (Digital Video Broadcasting) standards: by using specialized NIUs implementing DVB cable [4] and/or satellite [5] specifications, the user should be able to access, through the same system and the same graphical interface, broadcast programs and bouquets. In this environment the Service Information defined by DVB [6] and supported in DAVIC 1.0 should be exploited for navigation purposes.

References

1. ATM Forum, ATM User—Network Interface Specification 3.0, 1993.
2. ATM Forum, Audio-visual Multimedia Services: Video on Demand Implementation Agreement 1.0, 1995.
3. Digital Audio-Visual Council, DAVIC 1.0 Specifications, 1995.
4. ETSI ETS 300 429; Digital broadcasting systems for television, sound and data services—Framing structure, channel coding and modulation for cable systems, 1994.
5. ETSI ETS 300 421; Digital broadcasting systems for television, sound and data services—Framing structure, channel coding and modulation for 11/12 Ghz satellite services, 1994.
6. ETSI prETS 300 468; Digital broadcasting systems for television, sound and data services—specification for service information (SI) in Digital Video Broadcasting (DVB) systems, 1996.
7. ISO/IEC Draft International Standard 13522-5; Information technology—coding of multimedia and hypermedia information, Part 5: Support for Base-Level Interactive Applications 1995.
8. ISO/IEC International Standard 13818-6; Information technology—Generic coding of moving pictures and associated audio information, Part 6: Digital Storage Media Command and Control, 1996.

9. J. Heinanen, Request for Comments 1483: Multiprotocol Encapsulation over ATM Adaptation Layer 5, 1993.
10. M. Laubach, Request for Comments 1577: Classical IP and ARP over ATM 1994.
11. Object Management Group; The Common Object Request Broker Architecture, Revision 2.0, 1995.

Stefano Dal Lago received the Electronic Engineering Degree cum Laude from the Politecnico of Torino in February 1988.

In 1990 he joined Aeritalia—Space Systems Group where he contributed to the specification and planning of operations for electrical subsystems and payloads.

Since 1991 he is with CSELT where he is involved in the specification and design of image and sound terminal equipment for advanced communications applications, as well as in the preparation of experimental platforms for testing interactive multimedia services over various types of network. In this area he acted as CSELT responsible in various European R&D projects and co-ordinated CSELT's participation in specification and testing activities of the DAVIC Interoperability Sub-Committee.

At CSELT he is currently with the "Image Terminals" Research Unit, in the "End-User Services" Department.

Guido Franceschini received the Electronic Engineering Degree cum Laude from the Politecnico of Torino in October 1989.

In 1990 he joined CSELT, where he was originally involved in building early ATM terminals, using transputer technology and developing a network driver for delivering IP traffic over ATM on a SUNOS-4 Operating System. He has been then involved in the preparation of a high quality video conferencing system, with a particular focus on the development of various network specific adaptations.

For the ARMIDA system, he implemented the video pump. He is currently acting as CSELT responsible for the EURESCOM P605-JUPITER project, aiming in particular at testing interoperability between DAVIC implementations. Since 1994 he has been participating to the ISO/IEC Moving Picture Expert Group, to work on the MPEG-2 Systems and then on the MPEG-2 DSMCC specifications. Since 1994 he has been also participating to the ATM Forum, in the Service Aspects and Applications group.

At CSELT he is currently with the "Multimedia Applications" Research Unit, in the "End-User Services" Department.

Pietro Marchisio received a Computer Science Degree from the Università di Torino in 1983.

Since 1983 he has been with CSELT where he was involved in research activities related to database, object-oriented and user interface aspects. He led the design of user interfaces for telematic services and for public telephone network management systems.

He was involved in the ISO/IEC MHEG standardisation process and he is currently responsible for the development of tools and applications based on MHEG, with particular emphasis on multimedia authoring.

At CSELT he is currently with the "Multimedia Applications" Research Unit, in the "End-User Services" Department.

Marco Mesturino received a Computer Science Degree in 1989, and he has been with CSELT ever since.

At CSELT he was first concerned with software for automated VSLI design as well as software quality and metrics, contributing to various ISO/IEC standards on software measurement.

In 1993 he joined the "Multimedia Applications" Research Unit, in the "End-User Services" Department, where he is currently involved in SW-engineering, webbing, Jack-O'Unix, groupware, and bringing multimedia and decent bandwith to the Internet.

Enrico Polese received a Computer Science Degree from the Università di Torino in July 1990.

He joined CSELT ("End-User Services" Department—"Image Processing" Research Unit) at the end of 1991 where he participated in the design and evaluation of terminal architectures for interactive multimedia services and

H.320 videoconferencing over ISDN networks. He is with the "Multimedia Applications" Research Unit since the beginning of 1995, working on system study and design of user terminals, based on a PC platform, complying to DAVIC 1.0 specifications.

His current interest is mainly for advanced multimedia services, object-oriented matters and distributed systems.

Giovanni Venuti received the Electronic Engineering Degree from the Politecnico to Torino in December 1982 with a thesis on packet switched networks.

He joined CSELT in November 1984, where he was initially concerned with the implementation of real time automatic speech recognition systems.

Since 1988 he has been involved in the field of multimedia services and applications for Broadband ISDN. In this area he has been Project Responsible for CSELT in various national and European R&D projects.

At CSELT he is currenly Head of the "Multimedia Applications" Research Unit, in the "End-User Services" Department.

Multimedia Tools and Applications 5, 147–159 (1997)

An Interoperability Test-Bed and Test Results for DAVIC 1.0 Specification

HIDENORI OKUDA okuda@nttvdt.hil.ntt.co.jp
MASAHIRO MORINAGA, HISASHI KASAHARA AND KAZUNORI SHIMAMURA
Corresponding address: Visual Communication Lab., Human Interface Labs., Nippon Telegraph and Telephone Corporation, 1-1 Hikarinooka, Yokosuka, Kanagawa 239, Japan.

Abstract. This paper describes design and implementation of an interoperability test-bed for the Digital Audio-Visual Council (DAVIC) 1.0 specification. The system was designed particularly to test end-to-end interfaces and protocols between a set-top unit (STU) and a server. Using the test-bed, NTT participated in two interoperability test events, which were held together with several companies in 1995 and 1996. This paper also outlines those activities and summarizes the findings.

Keywords: DAVIC, interoperability test, test-bed, audio-visual applications

1. Introduction

The Digital Audio-Visual Council (DAVIC) is a non-profit organization in charge of specifying the open interfaces and protocols for interoperable digital audio-visual applications and services. The target applications are spread widely from digital broadcasting to highly interactive multimedia applications such as home shopping.

The spirit of DAVIC exists in accomplishing total interoperability of an application and the specification consists of various tools, each of which belongs to a different technical domain. Due to such multi-domain nature, there may exist inconsistency or holes from the system perspective. Furthermore, although each tool is specified carefully by the experts of that domain, there may be unpredictable defects in terms of interoperability. To remove such potential problems, DAVIC has encouraged the membership to exercise interoperability tests, where tools are actually put together into a system serving an application. To advance such activity, NTT has developed an interoperability test-bed and carried out interoperability test events with several member companies in 1995 and 1996. Some of test results were already fed-back to DAVIC and reflected in the DAVIC 1.0 specification [6] that was published in January 1996.

This paper elaborates the design and the implementation of the test-bed. The interoperability test events, wherein the test-bed was used, and the findings are also described. If readers are unfamiliar with the DAVIC 1.0 specification, it is suggested to read another overview paper in this journal or [2].

2. The scope of the test-bed

The DAVIC 1.0 specification consists of many tools. Our test-bed was designed particularly to test the following issues.

1. *Interoperability at* A1 *and* A9 *reference points.* DAVIC specifies interfaces and protocols at reference points, where the components implemented by different vendors may be connected in a physical or logical sense. Considering the potential of multi-vendor connection and the significance, we focused on A1 and A9 reference points, which reside between the set–top unit (STU) and delivery system, and between the delivery system and server, respectively.
2. *Interoperability in* S1, S2 *and* S3 *flows.* At the reference points, five information flows are defined in the DAVIC 1.0 specification;

   S1: to carry digital audio-visual contents from a server to an STU,
   S2: to select a content and control the transfer,
   S3: to establish and release a logical association, i.e., a session, between the STU and server,
   S4: to establish and release a network connection between them, and
   S5: to maintain multiple machines remotely from a network management node.

   Among them, we primarily focused on the end-to-end information flows, S1 and S2, which are essential for interactive audio-visual applications. S3 flow is also incorporated to carry initial information establishing S1 and S2 flows. The others were not examined in our test-bed.
3. *Interoperability in end-to-end ATM networks.* The DAVIC 1.0 specification defines several physical interfaces at the A1 reference point; for example, Hybrid-Fibre Coax networks, Asymmetric Digital Subscriber Line networks and end-to-end ATM networks. Among them, we particularly focused on interoperability in end-to-end ATM networks, which consist of ATM core networks and ATM access networks.
4. *Interoperability in mono-media retrieving.* As the basis of interactive applications, we focused on mono-media retrieval, where a single media component is transported from a remote site, interpreted by a decoder, and presented on an output device. Although DAVIC decided to use MHEG-5 to achieve the integrated retrieval of multi-media component, it is not incorporated in our test-bed. This subject is reserved for future activities.

3. System description

Our interoperability test-bed was developed in accordance with the scope described in the previous section. The overall system architecture is shown in figure 1. The system consists of three detachable components; a server, a delivery system and an STU. The components developed by other vendors were connected to ours at the A1 or A9 point in the interoperability tests.

3.1. Operation modes of the server and the STU

Our system supports S1 flow for carrying contents, S2 flow for end-to-end interactions and S3 flow for session control. However, a vendor interested in a less interactive application, e.g., digital broadcasting, might implement only the S1 flow in their system. If our system always required S2 and S3 flow, we would lose the opportunity of engaging in tests with them. To perform the tests with such vendors, our server and STU are provided with three operation modes.

Table 1. Features of operation modes.

Mode	Testable flows	End-to-end interactions	Session control
Mode I	S1, S2, S3	DSM-CC UU	DSM-CC UN
Mode II	S1	HTTP	N/A
Mode III	S1	N/A	N/A

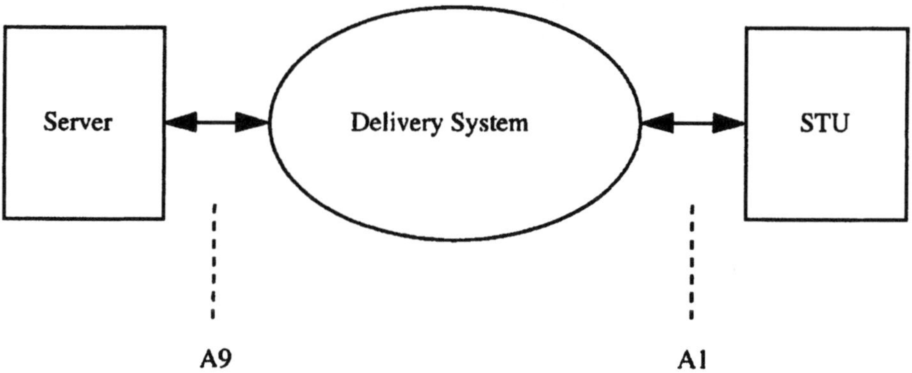

Figure 1. Overall system architecture.

Table 1 summarizes their features. Mode I supports DAVIC 1.0-compliant S1, S2 and S3 flows. It enables complete testing of end-to-end interoperability, whereas only S1 flow is testable in the other modes.

Mode II uses Hypertext Transfer Protocol (HTTP) for server/STU interactions instead of Digital Storage Media Command and Control (DSM-CC). The STU submits a completed form to the server for a directory query or a stream/file control. The HTTP daemon on the server passes the request to a service module through the Common Gateway Interface (CGI) and sends back the response in a Hypertext Markup Language (HTML) document. Although HTTP does not comply with the DAVIC 1.0 specification, the interactivity will promote S1 flow testing. It is also feasible since most vendors implement their test-bed on a WWW-aware workstation or personal computer.

In Mode III, no interaction is provided between the STU and server. Everything is self-controlled by the server. The STU works just like a passive TV set. This mode is used when other vendor's system is neither DSM-CC or HTTP aware.

3.2. Protocol stacks

In accordance with operation modes, the test-bed has three types in the protocol stack at A1 and A9. They are shown in figure 2. Although three operation modes use different stacks for the interaction flow, that of S1 flow is in common. Since the high-level API, i.e., MHEG-5, is not implemented in our system, the application program on the STU directly invokes DSM-CC User-to-User (UU) primitives in Mode I.

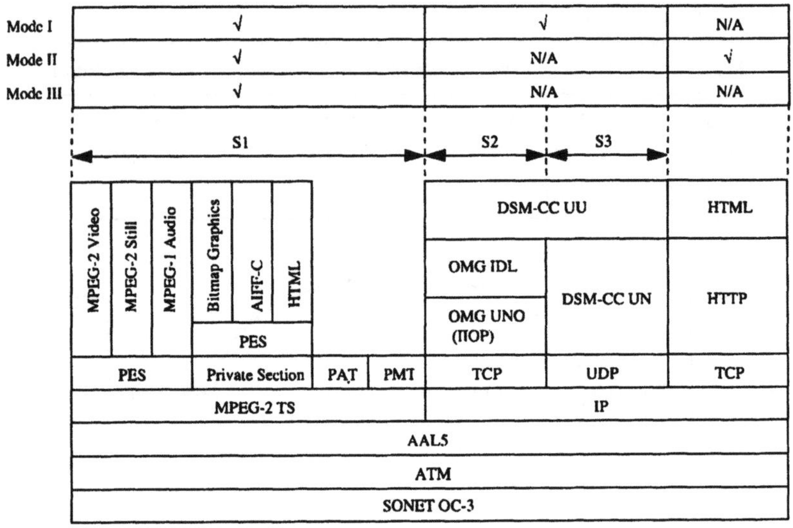

Figure 2. Protocol stacks at A1 and A9.

1. S1 *flow.* This is common in all operation modes. The test-bed supports six mono-media components; compressed video, compressed audio, linear audio, still picture, bitmap graphics and text. Their specifications are summarized in Table 2. The other mono-media such as service information is not supported.

   All mono-media are packetized into MPEG-2 Packetized Elementary Stream (PES) packets and carried by an MPEG-2 Transport Stream (TS). Although PES packets of video, compressed audio and still picture are directly mapped over MPEG-2 TS packets, those of bitmap graphics, linear audio and text are mapped into the Private Sections of the TS. Program Association Table (PAT) and Program Map Table (PMT) carry Packet ID (PID) information. Two TS packets are mapped onto an AAL5 PDU, and carried by eight ATM cells.
2. S2 *flow.* This is supported in Mode I. An STU-side application program makes function calls to the DSM-CC library. Each function corresponds to a primitive defined in DSM-CC UU specification. Our implementation is based on Committee Draft, which was the latest specification when our project was launched.

Table 2. Specifications of mono-media components.

Type of media	Specification
Compressed video	MPEG-2 MP@ML
Compressed audio	MPEG-1 Layer I/II
Linear audio	AIFF-C (no compression)
Still picture	MPEG-2 I frame
Bitmap graphics	DAVIC 1.0 Original (CLUT4, CLUT8 only)
Text	HTML

Table 3. DSM-CC UU primitives supported.

Interface	Primitives
Directory	close() get() open()
Stream	pause() play() resume() status() jump()
File	read()
Service gateway	attach() detach()

The primitive set is listed in Table 3. The underlying protocol is Internet Inter-ORB Protocol (IIOP) for directory, stream and file primitives. Service gateway primitives are handled in the different manner as described later. Since an Interface Definition Language (IDL) compiler was not available to our platform at the time of development, the IDL definition of each primitive was manually converted to the C++ code.

3. S3 *flow.* This is supported in Mode I. The STU interacts with the server via the Session and Resource Manager (SRM). The SRM is an intermediary agent in the network to maintain a session between the STU and server. It also allocates network resources to the session. The session setup sequence is started with "attach()" method of the local service gateway object on the STU. The messages that appear on the communication line are the corresponding Session Setup messages of DSM-CC User-to-Network (UN) specification. Once the session is established, the STU interacts with the server directly via S2 flow. To terminate the session, the application program calls "detach()" method and Session Release UN messages are exchanged.

   The underlying transport protocol of DSM-CC UN messages is UDP/IP at both A1 and A9 reference points, although the DAVIC 1.0 specification uses UDP/IP at A1 and TCP/IP at A9.
4. *HTTP-based end-to-end interaction flow.* This is supported in Mode II. As described before, HTML documents are used to carry interaction commands and responses instead of DSM-CC UU.

3.3. *Server*

The server is in charge of responding to the requests from an STU and pumping Transport Streams. The system architecture of Mode I is depicted in figure 3. The server is built on a UNIX workstation with an ATM-Network Interface Card (ATM-NIC). DSM-CC UN messages are received by a session manager. Once a session setup request message is received, the current session status is checked whether it is idle. If so, the session manager requests the application manager to start services for the STU. Since the server has capability

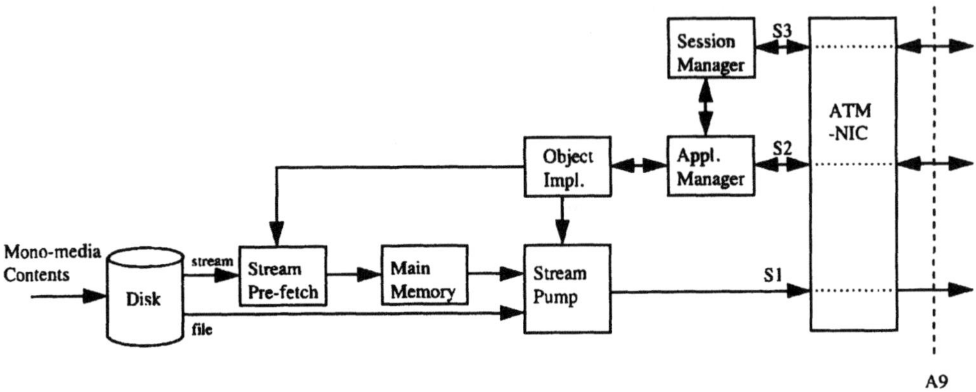

Figure 3. Server system architecure (Mode I).

of providing only one session at any one time, subsequent session requests will be rejected until the session finishes.

The application manager interacts with a service object in the object implementation in accordance with the DSM-CC UU primitive received from the STU. The object implementation is a collection of service objects, each of which implement some methods to provide services. In the object implementation, there exists three kinds of object; directory, stream and file. The stream objects support only basic VCR functions (play, pause and jump) at the normal speed and the file objects provide only the read function at present.

A video/audio/still picture segment is stored as series of MPEG-2 TS packet data in a file on the hard disk. When stream playback is requested, the corresponding TS packets are prefetched into the main memory from the hard disk. This buffering contributes to smooth pumping and makes it independent of any fluctuation in the access time of the second storage. Since we use general-purpose hard disks, the access time greatly fluctuates. The prefetched TS packets are sent out to the STU through the ATM-NIC. The stream pump module inserts PAT and PMT at the time of pumping.

The media other than video/audio/still picture are stored as raw data in the hard disk and packetized at run-time. These data are accessed when "read()" is requested on a file object. The file data are directly sent to the pumping module without going through the prefetching module, because file transfer can be bursty.

The server in Mode II has additional modules as shown in figure 4. The interactions with an STU are performed by HTTP instead of S2 and S3. The HTTP daemon drives CGI scripts to control the client simulator, which mimics DSM-CC client functions. The session manager and the application manager are connected to the client simulator instead of the ATM-NIC. In other words, S2 and S3 flows are looped inside the server and do not appear at A9. Obviously, this is a redundant architecture. However, it is effective in saving development time and expense.

Mode III is similar to Mode II except that the client simulator is controlled by a human operator instead of CGI scripts.

a) Mode II

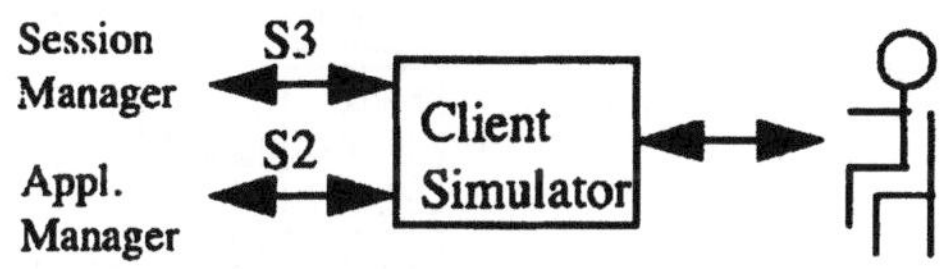

b) Mode III

Figure 4. Additional modules for Mode II and Mode III.

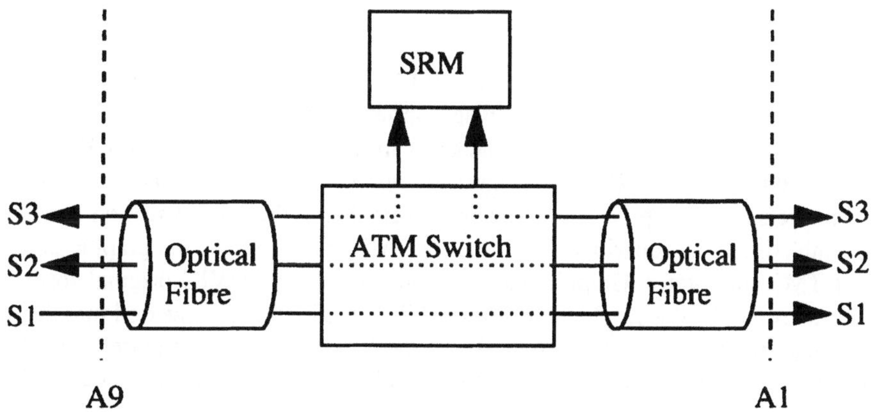

Figure 5. Delivery system architecture.

3.4. Delivery system

Our objective is to test interoperability in end-to-end ATM delivery systems. Therefore, the ATM interface appears at both A1 and A9 reference points.

The delivery system is an ATM network consisting of optical fibres, an ATM switch and an SRM. Figure 5 shows PVC connections in Mode I. There are four PVCs for a pair of STU and server; one for S1 flow, one for S2 flow, and two for S3 flow. Although S1 PVC is uni-directional, the others are bi-directional. Among them, only S3 PVCs are terminated at the SRM. At present, the SRM supports only a session set-up sequence and a session release sequence triggered by an STU. Other sequences are reserved for future development.

3.5. STU

The system architecture is illustrated in figure 6. The STU is constructed on a UNIX workstation with an ATM-NIC, an MPEG decoder card and a video overlay card. The

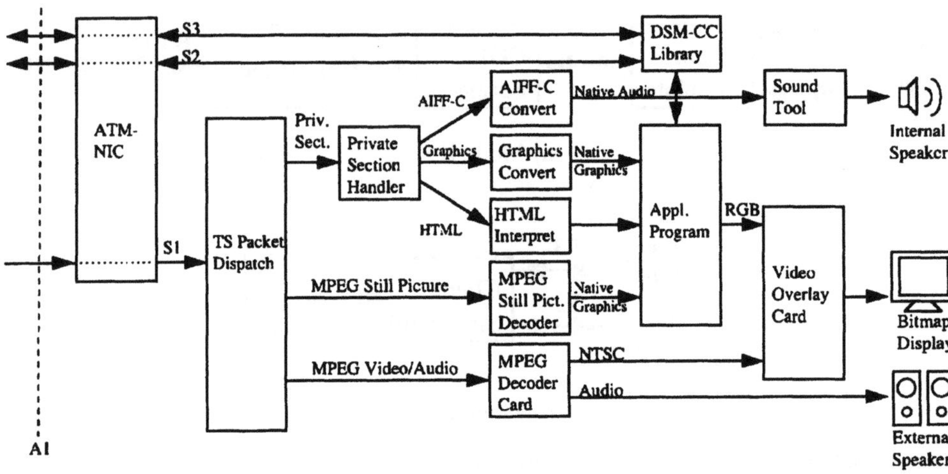

Figure 6. STU system architecture (Mode I).

ATM-NIC supports PVC connections. An MPEG-2 TS packet in an S1 channel is sent to the TS packet dispatcher and routed to an appropriate module depending on the PID, which is informed by PAT and PMT. The TS packets carrying MPEG-2 video or MPEG-1 audio are dispatched to the MPEG decoder card for system demux and decoding. Meanwhile, the TS packets carrying private sections are assembled at the private section handler and the assembled data are distributed to either the AIFF-C converter, the graphic converter, or the HTML interpreter. Graphic data are converted from DAVIC original format into X-window format by the graphic converter. AIFF-C audio is also converted into the native audio format by the AIFF-C converter. The TS packets carrying still pictures are delivered to the MPEG still picture decoder, because a single I-frame is too small to be handled by the MPEG decoder card. The application program provides a Motif-based graphical user interface for user interactions. The storyboard of the application is very simple; 1) establish a session with a server, 2) walk around server's directory structure, 3) select a stream or a file, 4) playback the stream or retrieve the file, and 5) close the session if requested. The X-window image is mixed with the decoded MPEG video picture by the video overlay card. Real-time graphics are super-imposed on the video window to simulate subtitling; non-real-time graphics are displayed in the independent windows.

Concerning interactions with a server, Mode I contains the DSM-CC library, which interacts with an SRM and a server. The functions in the DSM-CC library are invoked by the application program. In Mode II, a WWW browser is used for interaction with the server, instead of the DSM-CC library.

4. The interoperability tests and the findings

4.1. Outline of the tests

1. *Activities in Japan.* We organized an interoperability test group with several other Japanese companies in 1995 [4]. The objectives were to find any potential problems

in the draft of the DAVIC 1.0 specification and to reflect them in the final specification whose publication was scheduled in the end of that year. Through e-mail and face-to-face discussion, we identified some holes in the specification before commencing tests. Also, we made the decision concentrate on the S1 flows at A1 and A9, since some companies had not implemented DAVIC compliant S2 and S3 flows.

The tests were performed at NTT Yokosuka R & D center in November by six companies; Hitachi, KDD, Mitsubishi, NEC, Toshiba and NTT. They connected their STUs and servers with those developed by different companies. The focal points of the tests were,

a) MPEG-2 video encoding,
b) MPEG-1 audio encoding,
c) MPEG-2 TS, and
d) TS mapping over ATM.

The PIDs of TS packets were pre-allocated without using PMT and PAT, since some companies did not support them.

NTT participated in the tests by operating our STU and server in Mode III, which has no end-to-end interaction. The findings, which are summarized later in this paper, were reported at the DAVIC Berlin Meeting in December 1995 and reflected in the final DAVIC 1.0 specification.

2. *Interoperability event in New York.* DAVIC held an interoperability event at Columbia University, New York, in June 1996 [1]. The objectives are to confirm the DAVIC 1.0 specification and identify potential problems if any. The participants who provided STUs and servers were Columbia University, CSELT, DeTeBerkom, GCL, GTE, NIST and NTT. The tests covered the following interfaces and protocols;

a) MPEG-2 video encoding,
b) MPEG-1 audio encoding,
c) MPEG-2 TS, including tests of PAT and PMT,
d) TS mapping over ATM,
e) DSM-CC UU, and
f) MHEG-5.

NTT practiced tests a), b), c) and d) with other companies, using our STU and server. Due to a difference in the versions of DSM-CC and CORBA, we could not perform the interoperability test of DSM-CC UU. We could not test MHEG-5, either, since it was not implemented in our system. During the interoperability tests, our test-bed was operated in Mode II, which uses HTTP for end-to-end interactions with other companies.

4.2. The findings and discussion

The preliminary discussion and the interoperability test in Japan identified several problems concerning the draft of the DAVIC 1.0 specification and DAVIC responded to them as shown in Table 4 [3, 4].

Another noticeable finding was that the workstation-based servers could not produce the exact constant bit rate (CBR) streams without the aid of dedicated hardware. This deviation

Table 4. The problems identified by the Japanese interoperability test group.

Identified problems	DAVIC's responses
The well-known port number for S3 flow was not defined.	DAVIC became aware of this problem, but postponed defining a specific number. The number will be decided by an authority such as IETF.
The interval of PSI tables was not defined.	It was concluded to be out of scope, since it is a QoS issue.
Typical MPEG decoders do not have the capability of decoding Transport Streams at arbitrary bit rate.	DAVIC STU should be operated at any bit rate up to 51.84 Mbps.
The number of programs in a Transport Stream was not specified.	It was specified that a TS carries exactly one program in the end-to-end ATM case and may carry multiple programs in the non end-to-end ATM case.
There was no specification of assigning virtual channels for each information flow.	It was specified in Part 12.
The way of mapping IP over AAL5 was not specified.	LLC/SNAP encapsulation was specified as stated in RFC 1483.
A9 jitter was not defined.	It must be zero, i.e., no jitter at A9.

Table 5. The problems identified in the interoperability tests at New York.

Identified problems
Mapping two TS packets into a AAL-5 PDU is a hard task for a server. Performance would be improved if more TS packets are put into a PDU.
From the point or optimizing the server's pumping capability, it is desirable to define a discrete value for TS bitrate.
The precision of the constant bit rates needs to be specified to avoid buffer overflow/underflow at the STU-side due to bursty servers.

caused buffer underflow and overflow at the STU which was designed for precise CBR. Providing STUs with some amount of buffer to reduce the deviation of bit rate would raise interoperability with bursty servers.

The interoperability tests at New York also identified potential problems as shown in Table 5 [1]. These problems were presented at the DAVIC New York meeting for reflection in future activities.

5. Conclusion

In order to make the DAVIC 1.0 specification more complete, we developed an interoperability test-bed and examined the interfaces and protocols with other companies. The test results were fedback to the DAVIC community and some of them have already been reflected in the published specification. However, the interoperability tests performed to date were rather focused on S1 flow. In particular, we have no significant test results concerning S2 and S3 flows. Since they are essential for interactive applications, we need to make ongoing efforts on them, too.

The following are not explicit problems of the DAVIC 1.0 specification, but rather our findings or impressions after having experienced implementation and interoperability tests;

a) From the point of interoperability, the test-beds which implemented the specification strictly yielded worse results than loosely implemented ones. The latter systems are much tolerant than the former. For example, the STUs which use Presentation Time Stamp (PTS) for synchronizing audio and video sometimes showed worse quality than those without synchronization capability. Although they might be simply due to incorrect implementation, we need to prepare for such possibilities in raising interoperability.
b) The DAVIC 1.0 specification was created in the broadcast-centric way. That is, it requires heavy-duty service provider systems to make customer premises equipment as cheap as possible. For example, to reduce the memory size of client machines, the servers are required to keep the strict jitter specification which is difficult to achieve by general-purpose computers without a dedicated device. Although this approach does reduce end-customer device cost, server machines will cost more. To promote digital audio/visual services and applications, another approach, i.e., the peer-to-peer relationship of client and server, may also be necessary.

The goal of DAVIC is to define interfaces and protocols for interoperable digital audio-visual services and applications. In that sense, interoperability testing is a key activity in completing the specification. It would be our great pleasure if our work could contribute to advancing this activity.

References

1. H. Kalva, "Report of DAVIC VOD interoperability event at Columbia University," Workshop on Video on Demand Systems, Columbia University, June 24, 1996.
2. H. Kasahara, H. Okuda, and K. Shimamura, "DAVIC: Interoperability solution for video-on-demand systems," IEICE Trans. Inf. & Syst., Vol. E79-D, No. 6, June 1996.
3. M. Morinaga, H. Okuda, and H. Kasahara, "Tests of video-on-demand system based on DAVIC 1.0 specification," Proc. of 1996 IEICE General Conf., Vol. D-325, p. 123, 1996 (in Japanese).
4. M. Morinaga and H. Okuda, "DAVIC interop activities in Japan," Workshop on Video on Demand Systems, Columbia University, June 24, 1996.
5. H. Okuda, M. Morinaga, and H. Kasahara, "A test-bed of DAVIC 1.0 specifications," Proc. of 1996 IEICE General Conf., Vol. D-326, p. 124, 1996 (in Japanese).
6. The Digital Audio-Visual Council, "DAVIC 1.0 Specification," Jan. 1996.

Hidenori Okuda received the B.E. and M.E. degrees in precision machinery engineering from the University of Tokyo, Japan, in 1986 and 1988, respectively. In 1988 he joined Nippon Telegraph and Telephone Corp. and have involved in concurrent multi-video decoding and video-on-demand systems at NTT Human Interface

Laboratories. He received the M.S. degree in computer science from Stanford University, California, the U.S. in 1994. His research interests include human computer interaction, knowledge systems and visual communication systems. He is a member of IEEE, ACM, IEICE and ITEJ.

Masahiro Morinaga received the B.E. and M.E. degrees in electrical engineering from Seikei University, Japan, in 1986 and 1988, respectively. In 1988 he joined Nippon Telegraph and Telephone Corp. and worked on development of visual communication systems and medical image systems. Since 1995, he has worked on the reserch and development of digital video delivery at NTT Human Interface Laboratories. His research interests include digital video delivery and multimedia presentation. He is a member of ITEJ and IIEEJ.

Hisashi Kasahara received the B.E. and the M.E. degrees in electrical engineering from the University of Tokyo, Japan, in 1977 and 1979, respectively. In 1979, he joined Nippon Telegraph and Telephone Corp. and worked on the research and development of multimedia storage and retrieval systems. In 1986, he was a visiting researcher at University of Texas at Arlington, USA. Since 1994, he has been a senior research engineer and research group leader at Visual Communication Laboratory in NTT Human Interface Laboratories. His research interest includes digital video delivery and processing systems and settop computer technologies. He is currently the chairman of System Integration and Interoperability Technical Committee of DAVIC. He is a member of IEICE, IPSJ, ITEJ and IEEE.

Kazunori Shimamura received the B.E. and M.E. degrees in electrical engineering from Osaka University, Japan, in 1972 and 1974, respectively. In 1974 he joined Nippon Telegraph and Telephone Corp. and worked on visual communication systems, their interface evaluation and sophisticated teleconferencing. He received the D.E. degree from Osaka University in 1991. Since 1994, he had been the executive manager of Visual Communication Laboratory in NTT Human Interface Laboratories and is currently the executive manager of Malaysia Project in Business Communication Department, NTT. He is currently a member of Membership and Nominating Committee of DAVIC. He is a member of IEICE, ITEJ and IEEE.

Multimedia Tools and Applications, 5, 161–170 (1997)

A VoD Application Implemented in Java

ALEX DE JONG, KAREN HSING, DAVID SU {alex.dejong,karen.hsing,david.su}@nist.gov
Information Technology Laboratory, National Institute of Standards and Technology, Gaithersburg, MD 20899

Abstract. This article describes an implementation of a Video-on-Demand (VoD) system for the VoD interoperability test laboratory of the National Institute of Standards and Technology. It describes how Java can be used to implement the client side of a DAVIC based client-server system, which consists of a video server and a Set-Top Unit (STU) client. The communication between the video server and the STU is based on the Digital Storage Media Command and Control (DSM-CC) protocols. The VoD application is defined as a set of Java classes. These classes implement the graphical interfaces for user navigation and control. While this system is compliant with DAVIC specifications, it also permits an elegant integration of DAVIC services to the Internet environment.

Keywords: Video on Demand, Java, DSM-CC, DAVIC, Set-Top Unit

1. Introduction

A recent major advancement in information technology is in the creation, distribution, and use of information. The content of information has changed from simple text data to mixed information involving video, graphics, text, and audio. These information sources are available remotely from distributed hosts and service providers. Users interact with information through information appliances which may look like a personal computer or television set-top unit. The seamless transfer of information from content developers to information providers, to network access providers, and finally to users is a major issue for the success of any new application. It is important to address the interoperability issues at an early stage of technology development, particularly those issues that arise when users access information through appliances with various capabilities, and through networks from many service providers.

It is expected that digital video services will become a major business sector in the near future. The National Institute of Standards and Technology (NIST) has established programs to foster interoperability of products and services from this emerging industry. NIST has set up an interoperability test laboratory for the Video-on-Demand (VoD) service, one of many digital video services. This laboratory allows vendors to test the interoperability of their products with NIST's standards-conforming implementations as well as other vendor's products. As part of this activity, NIST is undertaking two major tasks: 1) development of a VoD reference implementation to facilitate testing, and 2) development of test methods for interoperability testing. The VoD service is based on the specifications of the Digital Audio-Video Council (DAVIC), an international consortium to develop implementation agreements for digital video applications.

"Video on Demand" means many different things to different people. In this article, VoD refers to a network delivered video service that offers the functionality of a home VCR (as a player only). By using a set-top unit, the service provides the users/consumers the ability to: 1) find and select a content item (e.g., a movie), and 2) interactively manage the viewing of the content such as fast forward, pause and resume the displaying of a movie. The first functionality is referred to as "navigation" and the second one "control".

In addition to this basic functionality, the service may provide the users a choice of a language for audio and/or sub-titles (called presentation control by DAVIC). Functions that enable loading/removal of the content to/from the service for the providers are certainly required. Before entering VoD, a user should be able to make a selection of a service and a service provider. The list is by no means exhaustive. NIST's VoD reference implementation initially focuses on a set of selected core functions to perform navigation and control.

This article describes the development of the VoD application at the client side of NIST's VoD system which is based on a client-server architecture. Section 2 depicts the model of VoD systems and the protocol stacks included in this model as defined by DAVIC. Section 3 describes why Java is chosen to implement the VoD application and how DAVIC systems can be integrated with Internet. Sections 4 and 5 present the design of this VoD application and a sample implementation using Java respectively. Section 6 presents the VoD testbed configuration at NIST.

2. Architecture Based on DAVIC

DAVIC has adopted a framework for interactive services which includes VoD[1]. A system is described in terms of reference points and information flows as shown in figure 1. The model includes a Service Provider System (SPS) and a Service Consumer System (SCS)[1] connected via a delivery system. For a VoD system, the SPS corresponds to the video server while the Set-Top Unit (STU) corresponds to the SCS. Between the server and the STU several reference points (only A1 and A9 are shown) and information flows (e.g. S1 through S4) are defined. The information flows enable the connection/session set-up/tear-down (S3/S4), and the exchange of control information (S2) and data (S1).

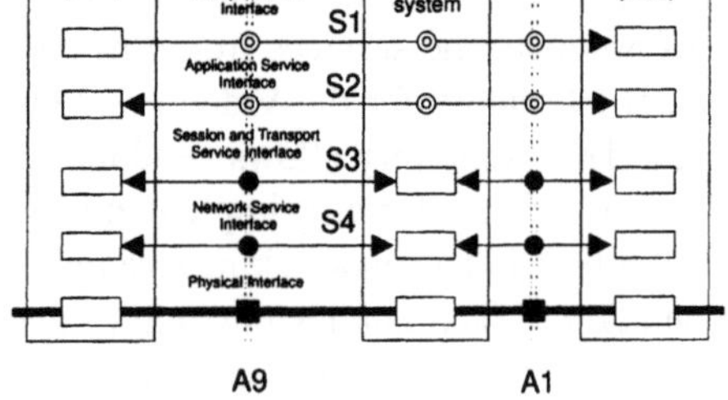

Figure 1. General DAVIC Model

After initial connection set-up and configuration of the STU–via DSM-CC User-to-Network (U-N) [2]–the DSM-CC User-to-User (U-U) protocol stack enables reliable exchange of control information via the S2 information flow. A VoD application utilizes the services provided by the DSM-CC U-U protocol to implement the retrieval of information from the server to be used at the STU.

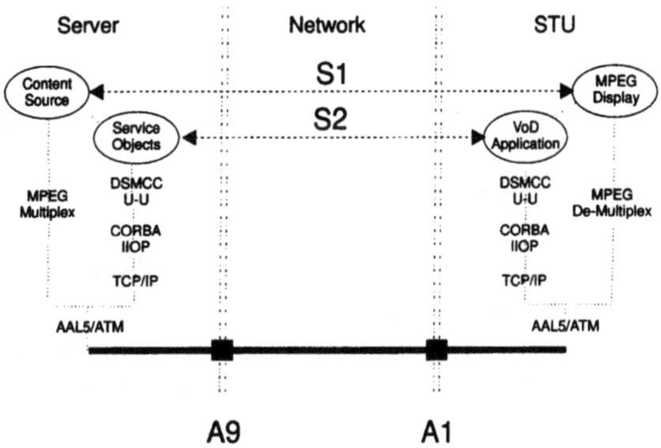

Figure 2. Video on Demand Model

Figure 2 shows a simplified model of an STU and a VoD server. Only information flows S1 and S2 are shown, including their full protocol stacks. The VoD application, which communicates with the server via information flow S2, uses the services provided by the DSM-CC U-U protocol. These services include *Session*, *File*, and *Directory* services. These services allow the VoD application to start a session and browse directories to retrieve files from the server. The files themselves can be used within the VoD application (e.g. images and bitmaps which comprise the user's interface).

Information flow S1 is used to carry MPEG 2 data. When a user selects to view a movie, an S1 connection is established (using information flow S3/S4 which is not discussed here) between the STUs and the VoD server. The STU's de-multiplexor/ decoding device handles the incoming data and displays it to the user.

3. Why Java?

Interoperability between VoD services and STUs from different manufacturers is currently limited because of a variety of incompatibilities. DAVIC describes a framework (see previous section) and has adopted standards for the communications layers, including the DSM-CC [2]. These efforts should lead to interoperable products in the future. Assuming that interoperability is ensured at this level, there is still the problem of interoperability at the application level. In order to run a VoD application on a variety of platforms, such as STUs running Operating System OS9 or more general workstations running a UNIX based OS, a VoD server has to create dedicated applications for each platform. An option, which is embraced by DAVIC, is to assume that the client implements an MHEG-5 engine [3] to interpret generic application descriptions. Because of the complexity of an MHEG-5 engine, this solution might not be economically feasible on low-cost STUs. Another solution, which is also being studied in DAVIC, is to utilize the popular Java language used within many World Wide Web (WWW) applications. Using Java to implement the VoD application provides the following advantages:

- Platform independent
- Dynamic object loading
- DAVIC and Internet integration

The Java language is based on the Virtual Machine (VM) concept. The intermediate byte code generated by the Java compiler is interpreted by a Java interpreter [2]. The Java byte code is platform independent. Because of the language's simplicity, the interpreter can be kept relatively small. The basic Java interpreter is only 40 Kbytes in size; an additional 175 Kbytes is required to include basic standard libraries [4]. This makes Java an ideal solution to provide graphical interfaces for STUs with limited resources (up to 4 MBytes of memory) while working just as well on high end workstations with virtually unlimited memory (16 Mbytes or more and hard disk space far beyond this).

Since Java byte code is interpreted at run-time, dynamic additions of code to the run-time environment are relatively easy to implement. This means that an STU only has to retrieve objects that it needs to initiate a particular piece of an application while remaining objects are retrieved whenever they are required.

DAVIC specifications 1.1 already include direct Internet access. This means that a DAVIC based STU can access the Internet in addition to DAVIC based servers. Java enables the use of the popular Internet browsers to access DAVIC based servers. Products are already available that enable Java integration with a Common Object Request Broker Architecture (CORBA). An Internet user can access a service provider by its Universal Resource Locator (URL); after which a Java applet is invoked. This applet in itself is a CORBA client which allows seamless integration between Internet and DAVIC based services[3].

4. Design of the VoD Application

The VoD server consists of a server directory structure which contains: movie streams, Java objects implementing the user menus and interfaces, and bitmaps/ graphics files used within the interfaces. Users connect their STU to the server, either by using an Internet browser (and starting an Applet) or a small dedicated Java program (which could be obtained via the DSM-CC *Download* protocol [2]) to obtain the initial application: *Init*. The *Init* application enables the user to attach to a VoD server via the DSM-CC *Session* service and obtain the actual VoD application by invoking *File* and *Directory* services.

The VoD program, depicted in the shaded area of Figure 3, is built on the DSM-CC U-U services. The upper half consists of 2 components: a static *Init* component that performs initial connection set-up, and the actual VoD program. Note that only the *Init* component resides on the client before a session has been established. The VoD program which implements user menus is loaded from the server dynamically, which allows a service provider to change the program without changing anything at the client side.

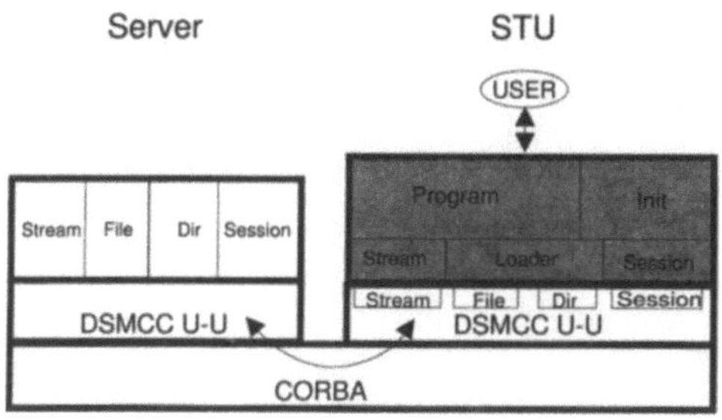

Figure 3. VoD application architecture

The *Session* component at application level provides attach and detach functions for *Init*. These functions are mapped directly into DSM-CC U-U *session* calls. The loader implements file retrieval functions for classes as well as data. Classes will be retrieved from the server and added to the run-time environment dynamically. Data files such as bitmaps and graphics can be retrieved for use by the program. The loader uses *File* service to retrieve requested information together with the *Directory* service to open/close directories on the server. A stream interface is layered directly on the *Stream* service in order to control a stream. All stream functions are implemented as application actions which can be attached to a button click or some other user event.

The DSM-CC U-U library contains the stubs to access the *Session*, *Directory*, *File*, and *Stream* services as specified in [2]. The Common Object Request Broker Architecture (CORBA) provides the underlying communications between the server and STU. The client-side library stubs will be generated directly from the DSM-CC Interface Definition Language (IDL) specifications by the IDL compiler [5]. The objects that implement the DSM-CC services are executed on the server.

5. Implementation of VoD Program

The VoD program is implemented as a set of Java objects. Java uses the O-O methodology and includes a class (or object) library which contains basic data types and system input/output capabilities. A powerful set of graphical interface classes is also included. These graphical interface classes are extended with VoD specific classes, such as VCR "play" or "stop" buttons, to provide a powerful set of so-called base classes[4]. The base classes themselves do not implement an actual user interface but provide the components to be used in the Graphical User Interface (GUI).

The VoD GUI consists of derived classes that actually implement the VoD menus and are specific to the VoD server contents. Only a derived class needs to be implemented to cover the details of a particular menu. For example, an addition of a new movie to a VoD server normally requires a movie specific entry in one of the menus which gives the user detailed movie information (e.g. actors, short description, etc.). The generic base classes will be re-used when new movies are added to the movie database (or within a completely different application) and or not VoD content specific. The base classes implement a model that consists of: *objects* and *actions*.

```
class AppObject

    class AppObjectButton
    class AppObjectLabel
    class AppObjectEntry
    class AppObjectImage
```

Each *object* represents a graphical piece of information on the screen. The Java pseudo-code[5] for these classes is listed above. Simple examples of such objects are: button, label, image, etc. All objects share some common attributes such as background color and sensitivity of the object to mouse clicks. Each object can define an associated *action* when the object is selected (either by mouse movement or by clicking).

```
class AppAction

    class AppActionWindowNew
        class AppActionWindowQuit
        class AppActionStreamPlay
        class AppActionStreamPause
        class AppActionStreamResume
        class AppActionStreamStop
```

Actions implement a mechanism similar to call-backs in traditional GUI programming. The difference, however, is that every action is a class in itself (versus a function call). To associate an action with a button or graphics object, an action needs to be created and attached to an object. Whenever the object becomes activated, this action will be performed.

The application window class is intended to be used as a base class from which the VoD program classes are derived. The base application window class implements and manages the screen and the objects displayed on it. A simple example of a GUI with a background image and 2 buttons, *Continue* and *Quit*, can be denoted as follows:

An example of a VoD program implementation using the application base classes as explained above is shown in figure 4. The opening screen shows the user a *Continue* and a *Quit* button.

```
// my application class window derived from base class AppWindow
class MyApplication extends AppWindow {
public void init(){

    setTitle("My Application");
    add(AppObjectImage (0,0,"bg.gif"));
    add(AppObjectButton(10,35,"Continue", AppActionWindowNew( NextApp )));
    add(AppObjectButton(30,35, "Quit", AppActionWindowQuit()));

}
}

// the next window has only a Quit button
class NextApp extends AppWindow {
public void init(){

    setTitle("Next Window");
    add(AppObjectImage (0,0,"bg.gif"));
    add(AppObjectButton(10,35,"Quit", AppActionWindowQuit()));

}
}
```

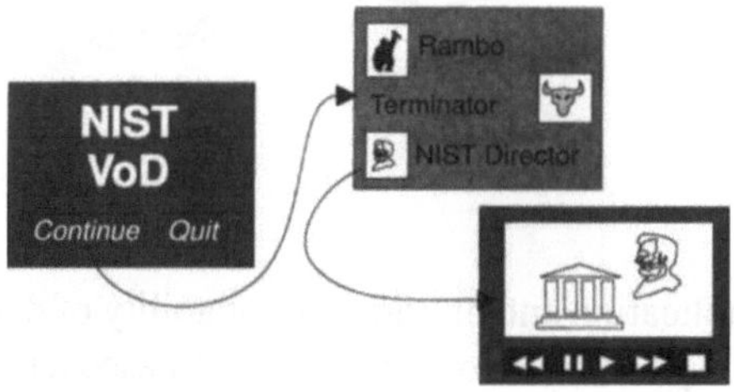

Figure 4. Example of a VoD program

After selecting *Continue*, a new window is shown which lists the movies available on the server. Each movie entry is listed with a preview picture and some additional information such as the movie title and actors. Selecting a movie opens up a VCR-like interface. It allows the user to start playing the movie, to fast forward, or invoke other common VCR playback functions.

Below is a list of classes that shows what is needed to implement the example shown in figure 4. Each class implements a window that can actually be displayed on the screen.

Upon user selection different windows are displayed to allow the user to browse the VoD server's contents.

```
class OpeningWindow
class MovieListingWindow
class VCRWindow
```

6. NIST VoD System

The Java approach as outlined in the previous sections is implemented in NIST's VoD system. The system consists of a VoD server and two STUs. The VoD server is configured with MPEG 2 storage space and delivery capability. NIST's server is a Unix based workstation with 16 GBytes of external disk storage for content (i.e. users menus and MPEG 2 Transport Streams). The server's DSM-CC is implemented using CORBA 2.0 . The system is connected to the Internet and an experimental optical fiber Asynchronous Transfer Mode (ATM) network, as shown in figure 5.

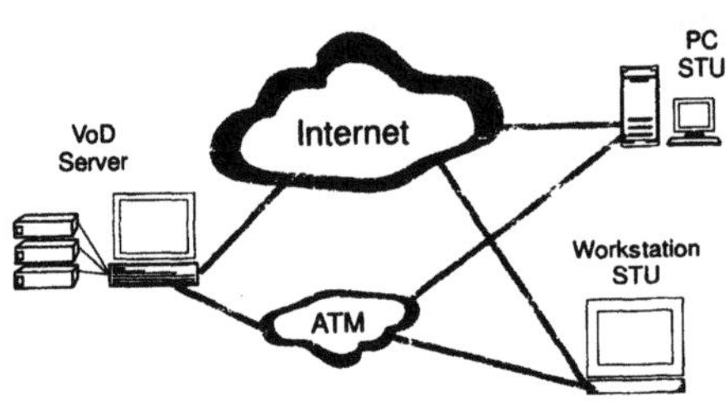

Figure 5. NIST VoD Testbed

The STUs run the VoD application and provide the capability of decoding and displaying MPEG 2 streams. Two STU systems demonstrate the Java based navigation and control. A complete software based STU[6] is implemented on a Unix workstation and a PC-STU uses a hardware decoder for MPEG 2 decoding.

A session with NIST's VoD server is established over the Internet with a WWW browser by simply selecting the VoD server's WWW home page. An applet that can be launched from the home page establishes the S2 control flow with the DAVIC based VoD server. If the STU does not have Internet capabilities but is a DAVIC compliant STU, the STU simply establishes an S2 control flow with the VoD server.

In both scenarios, after S2 flow establishment, the STU loads the server's *Init* program which, after execution, performs subsequent DSM-CC *File read* and *Directory open/resolve* operations to retrieve the VoD program–consisting of Java byte code and images–from the NIST VoD server. When executed on the STU, the retrieved byte code provides the user with menus for navigation and control. A simple menu could show the user the server's movie listing from which a selection can made. When a movie is selected for viewing, an S1 data flow is established from the server to the STU. A distributed stream pump implements the DSM-CC *Stream* state machine which handles transport of MPEG 2 data to the STU. The stream pump is capable of transporting MPEG 2 data over the Internet protocols and over the ATM network by using ATM Adaptation Layer 5 (AAL5)[6].

New movies can be added to NIST's server by uploading them via the Internet (e.g. ftp) or DSM-CC protocols. Only some additional Java code (See the examples in the previous section) needs to be added to make the new movie appear in the VoD menus to provide the user with detailed movie information.

7. Summary

This article described the use of Java to implement a VoD application based on the DSM-CC standard. A short description of the DAVIC framework and a more detailed VoD model were introduced. The VoD program implements the user menus to provide navigation and control for the VoD service. Using the Java language to implement the VoD application provides several advantages. The first advantage is that Java is platform independent. Secondly, Java allows dynamic additions of objects to the runtime environment which reduces resource requirements on the STU. Thirdly, and most importantly, Java provides a means to integrate the still expanding popular Internet with DAVIC services.

An example is presented to demonstrate the feasibility of using Java to implement a VoD application. This VoD application is implemented as a demonstration prototype at NIST. The prototype is integrated with NIST's VoD testbed, which is connected to the Internet as well as an experimental ATM network. The VoD testbed provides the infrastructure for NIST's interoperability test laboratory.

Notes

1. The Content Provider System (CPS) which is part of the DAVIC model is not shown here.
2. The Java interpreter itself is platform dependent.
3. Bandwidth requirements are not taken into consideration.
4. The base classes could implement MHEG-5 classes. However, a simple VoD application does not need the flexibility of an MHEG-5 engine. Using a proprietary set of base classes provides more than enough flexibility for the service provider. Only interoperability of the Java interpreter is required to ensure proper functioning of an STU with multiple vendor's servers.
5. The pseudo-code included is based on general Object-Oriented concepts.
6. See "http://mace.ncsl.nist.gov/vod/mpeg2ts.html" for more information

References

1. DAVIC, DAVIC Specifications 1.0, December 1995.

2. ISO/IEC, Information Technology–Generic Coding of moving pictures and associated audio information, Digital Storage Media Command & Control, International Standard, ISO/IEC 13818-6, August 1996.
3. ISO/IEC, Information Technology–Support for Base-Level Interactive Applications, Coding of Multimedia and Hypermedia Information, Draft International Standard, ISO/IEC 13522-5, December 1995.
4. G. Cornell and C.S. Horstmann, Core Java, SunSoft, Sun Microsystems, Prentice Hall, 1996.
5. IONA, Orbix 2 Distributed Object Technology, Programming Guide, IONA Technologies Ltd., Release 2.0, August 1996.
6. ATM Forum, Audiovisual Multimedia Services: Video on Demand Specifications 1.0, January 1996.

Alex Theo de Jong has been a Computer Scientist at the National Institute of Standards and Technology (NIST) since September 1996. Previously, as a guest researcher at NIST he worked extensively on EDI for 3 years. Now with the Multimedia and Digital Video group, Alex has contributed significantly to the development of NIST's digital video interoperability laboratory. His expertise includes network architecture and digital video technology. Alex received a MS in Electrical Engineering in April, 1995, from the University of Twente, The Netherlands.

Karen Hsing is a Computer Scientist at the Information Technology Laboratory of National Institute of Standards and Technology. Her current research interest includes utilizing distributed computing and high speed networks for video applications with emphasis on interoperability issues. Karen received a M.S. in Computer Science from University of Massachusetts, Amherst, Mass. in June 1974.

David H. Su is manager of the High Speed Networks Technologies group at NIST. His main research interests are in protcol development, performance measurement, and testing of emerging network technologies. He received his Ph.D. in Computer Science from the Ohio State University.

Multimedia Tools and Applications 5, 171–184 (1997)

Columbia's VoD and Multimedia Research Testbed with Heterogeneous Network Support

SHIH-FU CHANG, ALEXANDROS ELEFTHERIADIS, DIMITRIS ANASTASSIOU, STEPHEN JACOBS, HARI KALVA AND JAVIER ZAMORA
Image and Advanced Television Laboratory, Department of Electrical Engineering, Columbia University, New York, NY 10027, USA

Abstract. This paper reports our progress in developing an advanced video-on-demand (VoD) testbed, which will be used to accommodate various multimedia research and applications such as Electronic News on Demand, Columbia's Video Course Network, and Digital Libraries. The testbed supports delivery of MPEG-2 audio/video stored as transport streams over various types of networks, e.g., ATM, Ethernet, and wireless. Both software and hardware video encoders/decoders are used in the testbed. A real-time video pump and a distributed application control protocol (MPEG-2's DSM-CC) have been incorporated. Hardware decoders and set-tops are being used to test wide-area video interoperability. Our VoD testbed also provides an advanced platform for implementing proof-of-concept prototypes of related research. Our current research focus covers video transmission with heterogeneous quality-of-service (QoS) provision, variable bitrate (VBR) traffic modeling, VBR server scheduling, video over Internet, and video transmission over IP-ATM hybrid networks. An important aim is to enhance interoperability. Accommodation of practical multimedia applications and interoperability testing with external VoD systems has also been undertaken.

Keywords: video on demand, interactive video, video interoperability, video servers, MPEG-2 video over ATM, Internet video

1. Introduction

At Columbia University, we are developing a VoD testbed with advanced features of video storage, coding, manipulation, transmission, and retrieval. The main objective is to use this testbed as a platform for state-of-the-art multimedia research and application development. Among the potential applications are Columbia's Electronic News System, Digital Libraries, Interactive Video Courses on Demand, and other interactive multimedia applications.

Development of advanced VoD systems has been a prominent subject in research as well as commercial trials of broadband interactive audio/visual services in industry. Although some economic issues still exist and prevent large-scale deployment of VoD and interactive video services, designing a full-function VoD system for general multimedia applications remains a critical technical challenge and requires extensive interdisciplinary research. Much related work has been reported in the literature. The VoD workshop held at Columbia University [23] includes informative discussion participated by many researchers involved in testbed development, commercial trials, and new media applications. Several special issues in the literature also include comprehensive information about the state of the art technology [19, 20]. Specific technical approaches for individual components can be found in various fields as well. For example, dedicated storage architectures for real-time multi-access have been studied in [2, 13, 22]. Systematic approaches to the design of video servers (VS) are reported in [8, 14, 21]. Innovative methods for indexing/searching images by image contents were addressed in [9, 11, 15, 25]. In addition, many field trials of VoD services using proprietary high-performance VS technologies have made news headlines. Lastly, a major international forum, DAVIC, has been active in specifying standards for critical protocols and interfaces for achieving interoperability between various audio-visual applications [5]. In June 1996, we organized the first international interoperability event to test interoperability among clients and servers developed by different organizations. A total of eight organizations participated in the event [4, 6]. Description of the test process and result is included in another paper in this special issue [12].

Our testbed has several features which distinguishes it from other testbeds. The most important feature is the support for heterogeneous networks. Our testbed supports delivery of multimedia information over ATM, wireless, and Ethernet. Connected to these networks are different types of clients with different quality requirements. We have digital set-top boxes that are connected to ATM networks to handle high quality video, PCs/workstations with hardware/software decoders, and mobile terminals with hardware/software decoding capabilities. The bitrate and quality of the delivered stream varies depending on the capabilities of the client. While hardware decoders connected to an ATM network can handle high quality video at very high bitrates, the software decoders and mobile clients have to settle for lower quality video at lower bitrates. This has influenced our server design. We have designed a server that supports all these different networks and quality requirements.

This paper provides details on the different components of our testbed, clients, server, networks, and content. Overall architecture and design goals are presented in Section 2. VoD clients are discussed in Section 3, server architecture and design issues in Section 4, network issues in Section 5, content encoding in Section 6, and finally related research activities are presented in Section 7.

2. Architecture and design considerations

Right from the outset our goal was to design a testbed that would serve as a vehicle to conduct research and supports different *classes* of users. Figure 1 shows the components of the testbed. Starting from the right, the end-users can be classified into 4 classes depending on their decoding capabilities and network connectivity. Class 1 users are located on campus and are connected to the campus Ethernet, class 2 users are located on campus and use mobile terminals, class 3 users are connected to the testbed via Internet, we classify them as remote users and class 4 users are connected via local or wide area ATM connections. Each of these classes require different QoS and are served by the same server. The wide area connectivity to GTE labs in the Boston area is used to understand the effects of video transmission over wide area networks.

Figure 2 shows the high level architecture of the testbed. The client shown can belong to any one of the 4 classes mentioned above. Each client maintains two connections to the server during a session. A bidirectional connection for user control and a unidirectional connection from server to the client for video delivery. The level 1 gateway functionality allows the clients to select a server before establishing a connection. When a client selects a server, it is connected to the application server which allows it to browse the directories available on

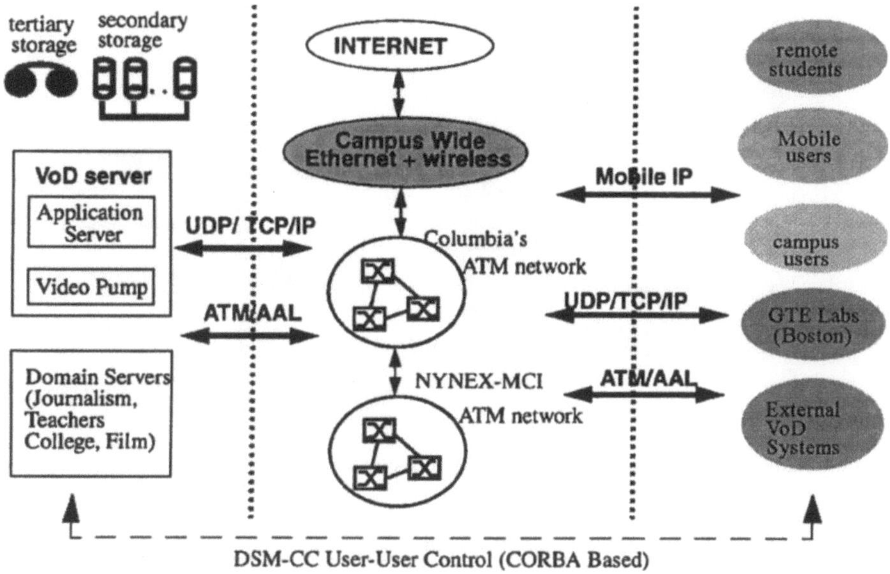

Figure 1. Components of Columbia's VoD testbed.

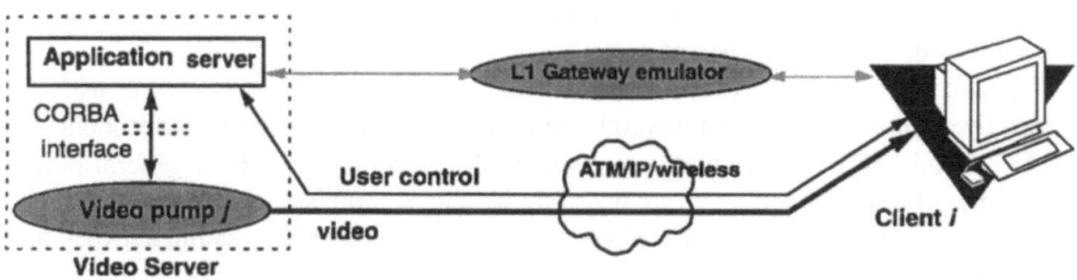

Figure 2. High-level system diagram of the testbed.

the server and select videos. Example functions and components in the application server includes Service Gateway, Directory Service, and File Service. When a video is selected, the application server invokes a video-pump process which delivers the selected video.

The envisioned applications include Interactive News on Demand and Video Courses on Demand. These applications stress the importance of real-time interactivity and multi-user access efficiency. The research issues driven by these applications are briefly discussed later on in Section 7.

3. Client

The client-side platforms may be composed of workstations, PCs, mobile terminals, or stand-alone set-tops. Both MPEG-1 and MPEG-2 decoders are already available for PCs and consumer electronics products. ATM adapters on workstations and PCs are also on the brink of wide proliferation. Due to the highly asymmetric complexity in MPEG coding

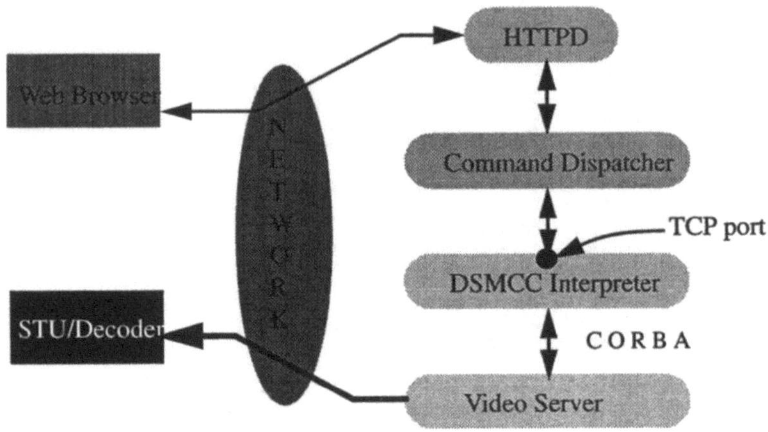

Figure 3. Control and data flow for clients with web-browser interfaces.

and multiplexing, the client side capability will not be a bottleneck in the end-to-end real-time data pumping chain. There are still some design issues, however, such as the trade-off between decoder complexity and scalable video coding, and the trade-off between the client-side buffer space and stream playback interactivity. These issues need to be investigated from a global, system-level perspective.

We have implemented software-based MPEG-2 decoder and playback routines with VCR interactive control functions on several workstation platforms. Hardware decoders (both MPEG-1 and MPEG-2 transport) are available for attachment to these general-purpose platforms. The mobile terminals are based on notebook computers with wireless Ethernet adapters and MPEG-2 decoders. Dedicated hardware set-tops with specific network interface modules are currently provided by external partners. In order to maintain maximal flexibility and extensibility, we focus on the general-purpose computing platforms at this stage. Thus, we do not require the use of real-time operating systems on the client side. As mentioned above, using the hardware transport stream decoders will reduce the processing load of the client computer and therefore may avoid the need of real-time operating systems.

To make the access simple and have a uniform user interface for all platforms, we have developed web-browser based client interfaces. Figure 3 shows the control and data flow paths between a server and a client with a web-browser interface. A user connects to a server by accessing a web page with a list of all the available servers. When a server is selected, the server ID is passed to the DSMCC interpreter by the command dispatcher. The DSMCC interpreter listens on a TCP port which does not change during a session. The information returned by the server, e.g., in response to the `directory::list` operation, is passed back to the client. When a video playback is requested, the video is delivered to the client directly by the server through the video pump.

For user interaction with the server we have adopted DSMCC [10] user-user primitives. DSMCC UU primitives allow a user to connect to a server, browse a server's directory hierarchy, select a service, make queries, and play videos interactively. We have implemented a subset of these primitives known as *core interfaces* that allow the users to connect to a server, browse directories, and play videos.

4. Server

Optimization of the overall VoD system performance requires a balanced system approach in exploring all the critical design factors for the video server. Fundamentally, it's a real-time data pumping problem—how to store massive video streams in a hierarchical storage unit (including memory, disk, tape, and tertiary storage), move them through the I/O interface and memory, and then pump them to the network interface. Careful data layout within the storage hierarchy, efficient real-time scheduling, and admission control mechanisms are all required in optimizing the system performance. We are investigating all these research issues in designing our video server.

Our server platform currently includes an SGI Onyx multiprocessor graphics computer as a super-server (with 6 CPUs and 1GB of memory), and clusters of workstations as distributed servers. The Onyx super-server is equipped with the high-end computing power and 3D-graphics capabilities that are needed in many interactive multimedia applications and real-time video manipulations. Dedicated disk array secondary storage is connected to the server, while local storage systems are available on distributed workstations. The server's communication interface is enhanced by the connection to an ATM LAN, which in turn is connected to an external ATM WAN.

The main components of the video server include a video pump for real-time CBR/VBR video stream retrieval, and an application server high-level control/management entity as shown in figure 2. The former is responsible for retrieving the video stream from the storage unit to the network and guarantee real-time performance. Our video pump is a generic design with support for different network interfaces (e.g., TCP/UDP/IP and ATM) and video types (e.g., MPEG-1 and MPEG-2). We take advantage of the multiprocessor architecture and the real-time process scheduling control of the Onyx machine to achieve real-time guarantees at a certain temporal granularity (e.g., 50 μs) [24]. For typical MPEG-2 video rates and ATM Service Data Unit (SDU) sizes, the temporal resolution at this level is sufficient.

The application server allows a user to select content and is responsible for forwarding the playback control commands such as pause and resume to the video pump. The application server and the video pump are two different software objects with a well-defined CORBA interface. This interface allows the application server to launch the video pump on a remote machine thus supporting a distributed video pump. Whenever a user selects to play a video stream, a new video pump process is launched. The video pump architecture is shown in figure 4. Each video pump object consists of three separate threads, one for control, reading and interpreting the commands from the application server, one for reading video data from the disk and one for writing data to the network. In the case of our video server, the reader and writer threads run on separate processors on the multiprocessor SGI-ONYX.

The video data is stored on the disks in the form of multiplexed MPEG-2 transport streams. The video pump reads this data and schedules the video packets for writing to the network interface. The scheduling schemes vary depending on the network types. In the case of ATM, two MPEG-2 transport stream packets are mapped to 8 ATM cells (AAL 5). The shorter PDU size significantly reduces the performance of the video pump. However an increase in the PDU size will result in an increase in PCR jitter. This increases the buffer size on the client to do de-jittering. This is a design trade-off which affects only the cost of hardware decoders. In the case of software decoders, the buffer size can be increased and

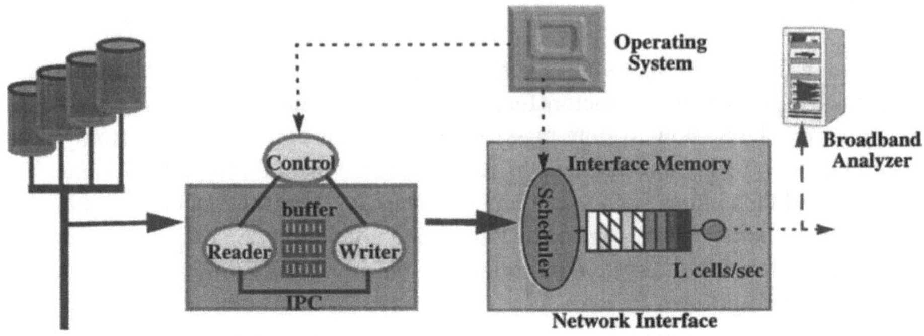

Figure 4. Video pump architecture.

hence the PDU size without affecting the end quality. The video server adjusts the PDU size depending on the client so as to keep the performance as high as possible.

5. Network

Our testbed is composed of different types of networks, ATM and IP. The ATM network is composed of four ATM switches and is connected to the ATM networks on medical, and Earth Science campuses. The network is connected to the external testbeds via NYNEX ATM network. We had a wide area connection to GTE labs during July–August 1996. This connection was used to study the effect of wide area networks and public ATM switches on the quality of video delivered. Studies were done specifically related to the measurement of cell delay variation and the effect of cell delay and cell loss on the perceived quality of the delivered video. All the measurements were made with the HP Broadband Analyzer and the network impairment module. In the case of the ATM network, the bidirectional control channel uses IP over ATM and video is delivered over ATM with AAL 5 adaptation.

The IP network is composed of Ethernet and wireless. The wireless network is composed of several wired-to-wireless gateways and supports mobile IP. The mobile terminals use a wireless Ethernet adapter with a maximum throughput of 2 Mbps. But video streams of up to 700 Kbps are used in mobile terminals as quality degrades at higher rates. For the user control information, TCP is used while UDP is used to deliver video to clients. The software decoders running on PCs can decode streams of up to 600 Kbps in real-time. To deliver video information at different rates for different classes of clients, a dynamic rate shaping (DRS) strategy is used [7]. DRS allows the server to reduce the bitrate of the video stream accordingly depending on the type of the network and the network conditions.

6. Content generation

All visual material is stored on the video server in a compressed form (e.g., MPEG-2 transport streams and MPEG-1 system streams). In order to reduce the time spent in content preparation, it is desirable to have fast encoding, packetization, and multiplexing tools. For live video production, real-time encoding facilities are required. We use an MPEG-2 hardware encoder (C-Cube) to compress audio and video. To multiplex the audio and video we rely on our software. We also use our software encoder to generate scalable MPEG-2 streams. Our software encoder and transport stream multiplexer currently run at a speeds lower than real time. The rapid advancement of today's computing technology, however, will hopefully resolve this problem soon. We should note that, for stored-video applications such as video on demand, an off-line non-real-time video coding facility is generally sufficient. For MPEG-1 video compression, a real-time hardware-based system hosted on a PC is utilized, generating MPEG-1 system streams (including both video and audio).

We have developed flexible software facilities for digitizing and encoding video from various sources (e.g., live camera, VCR, and LD player) and various domains (e.g., recorded lecture video, general movies, and test video from the public domain). Columbia's MPEG-2 software encoder (a full implementation, including all scalability profiles) is utilized to generate scalable MPEG-2 video streams while the MPEG-2 mux/demux software is used to packetize the elementary streams, and multiplex multiple packetized elementary streams (PES) to MPEG-2 transport streams. Timing information is captured by time stamps at different layers of the compressed bit streams, such as decoding time stamps, presentation time stamps, and program clock references, in order to maintain synchronization at different levels. Multimedia data such as text, graphics, and audio may be multiplexed into the transport streams as well, as described in the MPEG-2 system standard.

The bit rate allocation of each video stream depends on the type of the video source. In addition to the constant bit rate MPEG-2 main profile video streams, we also use hybrid scalable MPEG-2 coding to generate scalable video streams. We combine the spatial scalability and SNR scalability modes to produce three different layers of video. The base layer has a small spatial size and is suitable for video browsing and preview functionalities. The first enhancement layer increases the spatial size and keeps the video signal quality (i.e., SNR values) at a consistent level. The second enhancement layer improves the signal quality as well as the spatial resolution. Based on our preliminary and subjective evaluations, the base and first enhancement layers provide a subjective quality comparable to VHS video quality, while the highest layer provides a subjective quality comparable to that of a LaserDisc. The decision of whether to use scalable video coding or not should be based on the application types, system capacity, and encoder/decoder capabilities. There are currently no commercial scalable MPEG-2 hardware decoders available; scalability, however, is desirable in heterogeneous environments including different networks (wired and wireless), different client processing/display capabilities, and different user preferences.

7. Research issues

In addition to accommodating development of advanced multimedia applications, Columbia's VoD testbed also serves as an experimental environment for implementing proof-of-concept prototypes for advanced engineering research. The availability of an end-to-end comprehensive testbed is actually very critical to many research projects which have cross-disciplinary nature. For example, optimization of the video server storage unit cannot be isolated from research on video transmission over networks. There are strong interactions between the server scheduling/buffering mechanisms and network transport mechanisms. These interactions are best understood in an actual experimental testbed covering end-to-end components. We discuss several major research areas highly related to the VoD systems in the following sections.

7.1. *QoS guarantees in VoD services*

A key issue in a VoD service and in any video service is to provide an acceptable Quality of Service (QoS) to the end-user. This QoS is a function of many parameters, such as the frame loss frequency, blockiness effects, audio and video synchronization (lip synchronization), chroma stability (i.e., in NTSC display systems). Some of these parameters are not easily quantifiable since they depend on the subjective perception of the viewer. The QoS at the video client reflects how the original video stream has been delivered from the remote video server, where concepts of semantic transparency and time transparency characterize the performance of video services over networks. Such services require specific constraints regarding the delay, specifically the delay variation or jitter, experienced across the connection, as well as constraints regarding the rate of errors acceptable in order to have a guaranteed end-to-end QoS, from video server to video client. Therefore, an important question for VoD is how to map a specific QoS required in the video client into a QoS specification for the video server and network.

To answer this question, we have developed a novel and simple approach for mapping QoS from video server to video client, by using a generic model which can incorporate any VoD system [24]. We then provide an example of this methodology by applying it to the Columbia VoD testbed. The goal of our model is to provide an end-to-end QoS. In other words, we are examining how impairments in the video server, network and video client affect the quality of the video perceived by the end user. Since VoD is a point-to-point service, we provide QoS guarantees per individual stream rather than over an aggregate video traffic in the video server or network switch. Using this methodology we then derive an admissible region of traffic load in the video server which guarantees QoS end-to-end.

7.2. *VBR video retrieval scheduling*

Variable-bit-rate (VBR) video usually allows for better trade-off between video quality and network bandwidth. However it also demands more intelligent scheduling algorithms to guarantee the quality of service. In this research we investigate techniques to enhance our VoD testbed with video servers supporting both constant bit rate (CBR) and VBR *scalable* video. Our goal is to support heterogeneous clients and video interoperability.

In a generic model, the video server has a disk retrieval scheduler and a network stream scheduler. The disk retrieval scheduler determines how video data for multiple, concurrent video streams are to be transferred from the disk arrays to the memory buffers of each storage computer. The network stream scheduler determines how video data is to be transmitted from the memory buffers into the ATM switch for transmission to the clients. In our research, we found that the video server disk retrieval schedulers are critical in maximizing resource utilization for the retrieval of VBR video [16]. Note that the disk retrieval schedulers are different from disk head schedulers and operate over different time cycles.

Currently, we are investigating the network stream scheduler mechanism and also the interaction between the disk retrieval scheduler and the network stream scheduler. The network stream scheduler determines the transmission of stored VBR video over the ATM network. There is a fundamental difference between the transmission of stored VBR video for VoD applications and the transmission of real time VBR video for broadcast and conference applications. In our research we are maximizing the advantage of having a prior knowledge of the data trace of stored video to optimize the network stream scheduling.

In order to achieve maximal interoperability, we are investigating issues of scheduling real-time retrieval of scalable MPEG-2 video. We have developed a progressive display scheme, in which the video server supports different degrees of interactivity for the different layers of video.

7.3. Internet video

One of our current research effort is to enhance the interactive video service over Internet. Most techniques for developing video services in networks without QoS, i.e., Internet, involves an explicit attempt at avoiding network congestion. Clearly, network congestion hurts the performance for all users of the network. The goal is to send only the data that can fit into the network at a particular time. This requires an estimate of the bandwidth in the network. Much work has been done in the past regarding bandwidth estimation [1, 17]. However, providing good quality networked video requires innovative solutions from both the networking and image processing perspectives. Past attempts at solving the problem of video services over non-QoS networks have tried to isolate the problem as being purely networking. This has resulted in crude techniques, such as frame dropping, for forcing high bandwidth video streams through small bit pipes [3].

We are currently implementing a solution based on this dual-perspective approach. Namely, we are concerned with both the difficulties of bandwidth estimation as well as developing a methodology for shaping compressed MPEG-2 streams to a continuum of possible bandwidths. This technique is called Dynamic Rate Shaping (DRS) [7]. In its simplest form, DRS selectively drops coefficients from the bit stream which are least important in terms of image quality. This gives us the ability to dynamically change the bit rate of a pre-compressed stream.

7.4. Video transmission over IP-ATM hybrid networks

Another approach we take for developing advanced Internet video service deals with a realistic, hybrid network environment including both ATM and IP networks. Recent research on Internet audio and video service has resulted in a draft Internet standard for transporting real-time data known as Real Time Transport Protocol (RTP) [18].

We are using RTP and RTCP, the control protocol of RTP, to study quality of service issues in video transmission over hybrid networks. The RTP protocol has features to report packet loss and packet jitter to the source. This information in-turn will be used by the source to regulate the transmission rate by source flow control or source rate shaping described above. Another important issue is mapping of MPEG payload. A payload mapping should consider the packet loss inherent in the IP networks and support suitable error concealment and recovery schemes.

8. Conclusion

We have developed a state-of-the-art VoD testbed following a design approach that allows to have flexible components, while at the same time adapting to emerging open standards such as DAVIC. Our testbed was the central component of the global interoperability event organized here at Columbia University. With the campus-wide multimedia applications and video interoperability tests as the initial driving forces, we are building a VoD testbed with advanced capabilities of audiovisual representation/storage/retrieval/transmission. The testbed serves as an advanced prototyping platform for both engineering research and practical applications. It also facilitates the interaction between engineering researchers and application practitioners. Many practical applications are also being developed in this VoD testbed, including Columbia's Interactive Electronic News Experiment.

Our testbed has an entire spectrum of clients and networks and is very flexible to implement and validate new methodologies, algorithms, and applications. On the research side, our focus at this point covers innovative video server design, content-based video traffic modeling, heterogeneous QoS provision through multi-resolution coding and dynamic rate shaping algorithms, innovative compressed-domain video manipulation, and packet video transmission over ATM and IP networks.

Acknowledgments

We would like to acknowledge generous support for our testbed infrastructure from C-Cube, GTE Labs, HP-Idacom, IBM, NEC, NYNEX, and SGI.

The wide-area VoD interoperability test was completed jointly with the research group led by Dr. Leonard Ulbricht of GTE Labs. The DAVIC interoperability test was a collaborative effort with other participants described in [6].

We would like to acknowledge Xi Chen, Seungyup Paek, Paul Bocheck and other people involved in the Columbia VoD effort for their contributions to the testbed.

References

1. I. Busse, B. Deffner, and H. Schulzrinne, "Dynamic QoS control of multimedia applications based on RTP," in First International Workshop on High Speed Networks and Open Distributed Platforms, St. Petersburg, Russia, June 1995.
2. E. Chang and A. Zakhor, "Scalable video data placement on parallel disk arrays," SPIE Symposium on Imaging Technology, San Jose, 1994.
3. Z. Chen, S.M. Tan, R.H. Campbell, and Y. Li, "Real time video and audio in the World Wide Web," World Wide Web Journal, Vol. 1, Jan. 1996.
4. Columbia University, "DAVIC New York interoperability experiments: Report and results," DAVIC Contribution No. DAVIC/TC/SYS/96/09/008, Geneva, Switzerland, 1996.
5. DAVIC 1.0 Specification, The Digital Audio-Visual Council (DAVIC) 1995.
6. DAVIC VoD Interoperability Test Event, June 1996, Columbia University, New York. (http://www.itnm.columbia.edu/vod/interop96)
7. A. Eleftheriadis and D. Anastassiou, "Meeting arbitrary QoS constraints using dynamic rate shaping of coded digital video," Proceedings, 5th International Workshop on Network and Operating System Support for Digital Audio and Video (NOSSDAV-95), Durham, New Hampshire, April 1995, pp. 95–106.

8. C. Federighi and L.A. Rowe, "The design and implementation of the UCB distributed video on demand system," Proc. of IS&T/SPIE 1994 Int'l Symp. on Elec. Imaging: Science and Technology, San Jose, CA, Feb. 1994.
9. M. Flickner et al., "Query by image and video content: The QBIC system," IEEE Computer Magazine, Vol. 28, No. 9, pp. 23–32, Sept. 1995.
10. Generic Coding of Moving Pictures and Associated Audio (DSMCC), ISO/IEC 13818-6, International Standard, 1996.
11. A.G. Hauptmann and M. Smith, "Text, speech and vision for video segmentation: The informedia project," AAAI Fall Symposium, Computational Models for Integrating Language and Vision, Boston, Nov. 10–12, 1995.
12. H. Kalva, S.-F. Chang, and A. Eleftheriadis, "DAVIC and interoperability experiments," International Journal on Multimedia Tools and Applications, Kluwer Academic Publishers, 1997.
13. K. Keeton and R. Katz, "The evaluation of video layout strategies on a high-bandwidth file server," Intern. Workshop on Network and Operating System Support for Digital Audio and Video, Lancaster, England, UK, Nov. 1993.
14. T.D.C. Little, G. Ahanger, R.J. Folz, J.F. Gibbon, W.W. Reeve, D.H. Schelleng, and D. Venkatesh, "A digital on-demand video service supporting content-based queries," ACM 1st Multimedia Conference, Anaheim, CA, Aug. 1993.
15. J. Meng and S.-F. Chang, "CVEPS: A compressed video editing and parsing system," ACM Multimedia Conference, Boston, MA, Nov. 1996.
16. S. Paek and S.-F. Chang, "Video server retrieval scheduling for VBR scalable video," Third IEEE International Conference on Multimedia Computing & Systems, Japan, 1996.
17. T. Sakatani, "Congestion avoidance for video over IP networks," Multimedia Transport and Teleservices Proceedings, pp. 256–273, Nov. 13–15, 1994.
18. H. Schulzrinne, S. Casner, and R. Frederick, "RTP: A transport protocol for real-time applications," RFC 1889, Internet Engineering Task Force, Jan. 1996.
19. Special Issue on "Video on demand," IEEE Communications Magazine, Vol. 32, No. 5, May 1994.
20. Special Issue on "Video on demand," International Journal of Image Communication—Signal Processing, Vol. 8, No. 3, April 1996.
21. M. Vernick, C. Venkatramini, and T.-C. Chiueh, "Adventures in building the stony brook video server," ACM Multimedia Conference, Boston, MA, Nov. 1996.
22. H.M. Vin and P.V. Rangan, "Designing a multi-user HDTV storage server," IEEE Journal on Selected Areas in Communications, Vol. 11, No. 1, Jan. 1993.
23. Workshop on Video on Demand Systems—Technology, Interoperability, and Trials, Columbia University, June 1996. (http://www.itnm.columbia.edu/workshop/vod96).
24. J. Zamora, S. Jacobs, A. Eleftheriadis, S.-F. Chang, and D. Anastassiou, "A practical methodology for guaranteeing QoS for video on demand," submitted for publication, April 1996.
25. H. Zhang, C.Y. Low, and S. Smoliar, "Video parsing and browsing using compressed data," J. of Multimedia Tools and Applications, Kluwer Academic Publishers, Vol. 1, No. 1, pp. 89–111, March 1995.

Shih-Fu Chang is currently an Associate Professor at Department of Electrical Engineering and Center for Telecommunications Research in Columbia University. He received the M.S. and Ph.D. degree in Electrical Engineering and Computer Science from the University of California at Berkeley in 1991 and 1993, respectively.

Dr. Chang's current research interests include content-based image technologies for multimedia systems, visual information systems, and image/video signal processing and communications. At Columbia, he is co-leading the development of a Video-on-Demand/Multimedia Testbed, and Columbia's audio-visual service interoperability experiments. His group has developed several advanced prototypes in visual information systems, including an image/video search and cataloging engine, WebSEEk, and a Web-based compressed video editing and search system, CVEPS.

He was the recipient of the best paper award of SPIE International Symposium on Visual Communications and Image Processing 1995, the best student paper award of the ACM first Multimedia Conference 1993, an NSF CAREER award 1995–8, and an IBM University Research Partnership (Faculty Development) Award 1995–7. He serves on the editorial boards and program committees of several international conferences and publications. He was the organizer and co-chair of Workshop on Video on Demand Systems—Technology, Interoperability and Trials, held at Columbia University in June 1996.

Alexandros Eleftheriadis was born in Athens, Greece, in 1967. He received the Diploma in Electrical Engineering and Computer Science from the National Technical University of Athens, Greece, in 1990, and the M.S., M.Phil., and Ph.D. degrees in Electrical Engineering from Columbia University, New York, in 1992, 1994, and 1995 respectively.

Since 1995 he has been an Assistant Professor in the Department of Electrical Engineering at Columbia University, where he is leading a research team working in the areas of video signal processing and compression, video communication systems, distributed multimedia systems, and the fundamentals of compression. During the summers of 1993 and 1994, he was with AT&T Bell Laboratories, Murray Hill, NJ, developing low bit rate video coding techniques for videoconferencing applications. From 1990 until 1995, he was a Graduate Research Assistant in the Department of Electrical Engineering at Columbia University.

Prof. Eleftheriadis is a member of the ANSI X3L3.1 Committee, and is participating in the ISO/IEC JTC1/SC29/WG11 (MPEG) standardization activity as well as DAVIC. He is also a member of the IEEE, the ACM, and the Technical Chamber of Greece.

Dimitris Anastassiou was born in Athens, Greece, in 1952. He received the Diploma in electrical engineering from the National Technical University of Athens, Greece, in 1974, and the M.S. and Ph.D. degrees from the University of California, Berkeley, in 1975 and 1979, respectively.

He joined the faculty of Columbia University in 1983, where he is currently Professor of Electrical Engineering, Director of the Image and Advanced Television Laboratory, and Director of Columbia University's cross-disciplinary "New Media Technology Center."

Prior to joining Columbia University in 1983, he was with the IBM Thomas J. Watson Research Center, Yorktown Heights, NY, as a Research Staff Member, working on the development of the internal IBM videoconferencing system.

His research interests focus on digital video processing and communications, with emphasis on multimedia applications. He has received an IBM Outstanding Innovation Award and an NSF Presidential Young Investigator Award. He is an Associate Editor of the IEEE Transactions on Circuits and Systems for Video Technology, and a member of ISO's Moving Picture Experts Group (MPEG) digital video coding standardization effort. He has been Guest Editor of special issues for various journals and has co-organized MPEG and DAVIC meetings at Columbia University, as well as several workshops and sessions on the subject of digital video and Advanced Television.

Stephen Jacobs received the B.S. and M.S. in electrical engineering from Columbia University in 1994 and 1995, respectively. He also holds a B.A. in Physics from Bard College.

He is currently a Ph.D. candidate in the Electrical Engineering Department at Columbia University and a Graduate Research Assistant in the Image and Advanced Television Laboratory. His research interests include adaptive multimedia protocols and applications.

In 1996, Mr. Jacobs was awarded the Kodak Fellowship. He is a student member of the IEEE.

Hari Kalva received the B.Tech. degree from N.B.K.R. Institute to Science and Technology, S.V. University, Tirupati, India in 1991 and the M.S. from Florida Atlantic University, Boca Raton, FL in 1994.

From Jan. 1995 to Aug. 1996, he was a Research Staff Associate in the ADVENT project at Columbia University. He is currently a Ph.D. student in the Department of Electrical Engineering at Columbia University. His research interests include Multimedia Communication Systems and protocols.

Javier Zamora received the Telecommunications Engineering Degree in 1990 (B.S. and M.S.) from the Polytechnic University of Catalonia (UPC), Spain, with a specalization in Communications. He took part in several video and Television related projects with both SANYO and IBM. Afterwards, he carried research and academic positions at the Department of Applied Mathematics and Data Transmission (UPC).

He is currently a Ph.D. candidate in the Electrical Engineering Department at Columbia University and a Graduate Research Assistant in the Image Technology for New Media Center. His research interests include video-on-demand systems, ATM networks and quality of service issues.

Mr. Zamora was awarded the Catalonian Government and "la Caixa" Fellowships. He is a member of the IEEE and of the ATM Forum.

Multimedia Tools and Applications 5, 185–197 (1997)

The Video-On-Demand Trial in Taiwan: A Partially DAVIC Compliant System

YUAN-LIANG SU
KAE-JY CHOU choukj@panda.ccl.itri.org.tw
CHIH-WEN CHENG, JIN-JEN HSUE, FU-YUNG LAI, JUN-LIN LIU AND CHUN-I WANG
Computer & Communication Research Laboratories, Industrial Technology Research Institute, Bldg. 14, 195-11 Sec. 4, Chung Hsing Rd., Chutung, Hsinchu, Taiwan 310

Abstract. This paper reviews the Video-On-Demand technical trial conducted by Computer & Communication Research Laboratories in Taiwan. This trial is one of the key realization of Taiwan's National Information Infrastructure. The primary goal is to provide a testbed and platform for new product development, interoperability test, and interactive multimedia applications. It also explores the technical difficulties from which experiences can be gained for future large scale deployment. Open system and end-to-end system are the most important requirements of the VOD system in this trial. Open system allows a variety of video servers and set-top boxes to be integrated into the system while end-to-end system requires system integration know-how.

An overview of the Video-On-Demand system is provided in this paper. The architecture of the video server, delivery network and set-top box will be examined. The system integration issues including content preparation will also be discussed.

Keywords: Video-On-Demand (VOD), hybrid fiber coax (HFC), system integration

I. Introduction[1]

The Video-On-Demand (VOD) trial system which will serve 200 households has been conducted in the Science-Based Industrial Park, Hsinchu, Taiwan, ROC. It is an interactive, broadband large-scale technical trial conducted by Computer & Communication Research Laboratories (CCL), Industrial Technology Research Institute (ITRI). The VOD system enables a viewer to watch his/her favorite movies using a remote control unit at any time. It is one of the key realizations of Taiwan's National Information (NII) Infrastructure that provides real-time, broadband multimedia services. For the details of other trials, please refer to [1, 9].

The primary goal of this trial is to provide a testbed and platform for new product development, interoperability test, and interactive multimedia services. The trial is funded by the government to accelerate the progress of improving industry competence and to promote the research and development of interactive multimedia applications. It also explores the technical difficulties from which experiences can be gained for future large scale deployment. Open system and end-to-end system requirements are the most important specifications of the VOD system in this trial. Open system allows a variety of video servers and set-top boxes (STBs) to be integrated into the system. This multi-server, multi-set-top-box architecture provides the local computer and communication industries an opportunity to test and connect their products to the system. End-to-end system requires comprehensive system integration know-how. The aggregation of video servers, headend and STBs does not guarantee the success of the system. The designers have to consider all the system integration issues before the actual deployment.

In the following, Section II presents the CCL Video-On-Demand system in which each subsection addresses some specific topics. The specifications and the video delivery mechanism from the video server to the set-top box are described in the first two subsections. The third subsection reviews the hybrid fiber coax (HFC) network deployment in this trial and the last subsection introduces content preparation and video production. Section III discusses the system integration issues raised from this trial. Finally, Section IV concludes the discussion with the future plan.

II. VOD system

This section provides an overview of the CCL Video-On-Demand system as depicted in figure 1. It covers content creation, system architecture and implementation. The system consists of three major entities: video server, delivery network and set-top box. The video server can support 50 video streams and allow up to 20 users to access the same program concurrently. The delivery network comprises the headend and HFC access network. Video streams from the server are packetized into ATM (Asynchronous Transfer Mode) cells and are transported to the headend. After the ATM cells are modulated by the Quadrature Amplitude Modulation (QAM) and are combined with conventional analog CATV signal, the headend delivers the combined analog signal to the customers through the HFC network. The set-top box in the customer site extracts the MPEG-2 video from the ATM cells, decompresses the MPEG-2 video and communicates with the server interactively. See [2, 3, 6, 11] for more detail on the VOD design issues.

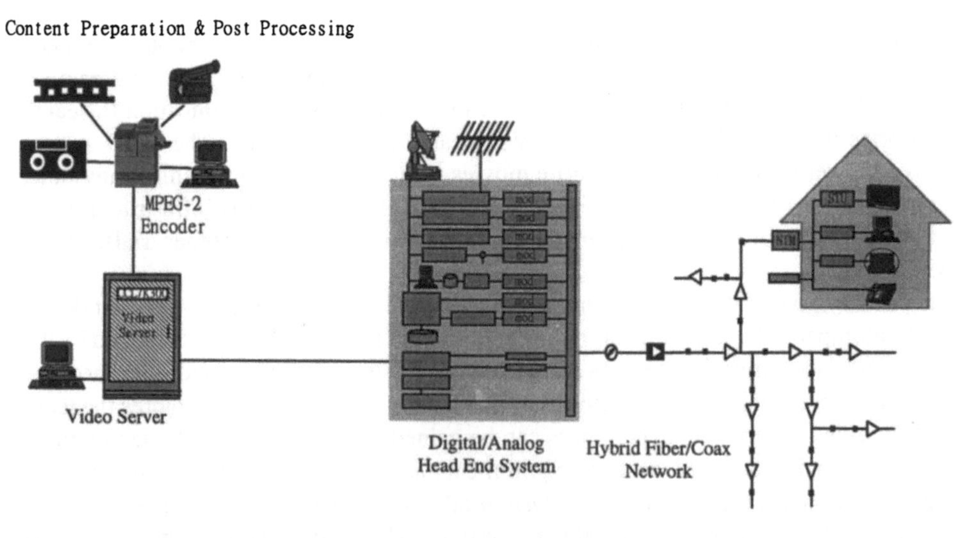

Figure 1. **VOD system architecture.**

A. *System specification*

The most important requirement in the VOD system specification is that the system shall be a true VOD system in the sense that a user has full control over the whole session [5]. For example, a user can pause, stop, resume, reverse and forward the video. It is different from the "Near VOD", which repetitively broadcasts the same program at, say, every 10 minutes. The NVOD gives the user an illusion that he/she can forward or reverse the program, yet it is a one-way broadcast system. The major features of each entity in the VOD system are described with a general introduction followed by the specific requirements.

1. Video server. A video server consists of storage devices and the control mechanism required to store movies in a compressed format and to play them back on request. The storage devices may be RAM, hard disks, tapes and MO disks. It differs from a traditional database server in many aspects. It has to perform a number of functions such as admission control, request handling, data retrieval, guaranteed stream transmission, stream encryption, and support of VCR-like functions. Another characteristic of a video server is that it supports many users to view the same program in different time instants. One way to support one program for many views is to have many identical copies of the program, each program serving one viewer. Another method is to use the technique of data striping that the video is divided into small chunks placed in different hard disks. When many users view the same program, or equivalently access the same video, the video server can simultaneously retrieve different chunks of the video from different hard disks.

The major features of the video server in this trial are:

Bandwidth: Support 50 streams @ 3 Mb/s.
Concurrence: Allow up to 20 users accessing the same program material concurrently.
Data transport:

(a) MPEG-2 transport stream.
(b) Capable of transporting MPEG-1 stream.

Data storage:

(a) Support 50 2-hour MPEG-2 movies.
(b) Hierarchical file system.

Network interface:

(a) ATM-based switch network.
(b) MPEG-2 transport stream carried over ATM cells by AAL5.

2. Delivery network. The delivery network includes the headend and access network. The main functionality of the headend is (1) to convert OC-3c ATM cells to QAM RF signals; (2) to establish connections with the video server and set-top boxes respectively; (3) to provide a communication link between the video server and set-top boxes.

In this trial, HFC network is chosen as the access network architecture. A typical HFC network delivers video services over a fiber optic network to a neighbourhood node, where optical to electrical conversion is done. The electrical signal is transported over a coax network to all users on that node. A multiple access mechanism needs to be implemented to provide interactivity. Return signals are converted to optical signals at the fiber node and sent back to the headend via another fiber.

The spectrum assignment for the HFC network is as follows:

(a) *Analog CATV broadcasting*: 50~550 MHz.
(b) *Digital VOD channels*: 550~750 MHz.
(c) *Upstream control signal*: 5~35 MHz.

The headend for this trial have the following capabilities:

(a) *Signal processing*: Provide switching/multiplexing/modulation functions.
(b) *Connection*: Establish and manage the transport connections between video server and STBs.
(c) *Menu*: Present subscribers a menu of available information providers.
(d) *Signal combination*: Combine digital video with analog CATV broadcasting.
(e) *Operation, administration and maintenance (OA&M)*: Provide basic OA&M functions such as resource allocation, network management etc.

3. Set-top box. The major task of a set-top box is to decompress the MPEG-2 data and to enable viewers to communicate with the server interactively [8]. The physical interface to the network is a coax cable connector where the transmission and receiving signals are handled by the line transceiver. An RF tuner is tuned to the assigned channel that carries the downstream data signal. The downstream data signal has to be demodulated, demultiplexed, decompressed and, then, modulated to the TV signal. A processor controlled by a real time operating system and application programs coordinate all the components to accomplish the desired task.

The STB for this trial has the following capabilities:

(a) *Audio decoding*: The basic format of audio data to be accepted by the STB is MPEG-1 or MPEG-2.
(b) *Video decoding*: The STB accepts and correctly processes MPEG-2(ISO/IEC 13818-2) Main Profile at Main Level video stream data. All data rates up to 10 Mb/s are supported by the decoding function of the STB.
(c) *Transport stream*: Synchronization of Audio/Video is done by MPEG-2 Transport Stream (ISO/IEC 13818-1).

B. Video delivery

The video delivery flow from the video server to STBs, or video downstream, is depicted in figure 2. The video is in MPEG-2 TS format and stored in the video server. When the user requests a movie, the server encapsulates MPEG-2 TS video into the 48-byte payload of the ATM cells with ATM Adaptation Layer 5 (AAL5) and sends to the 155 Mbps OC-3c optical

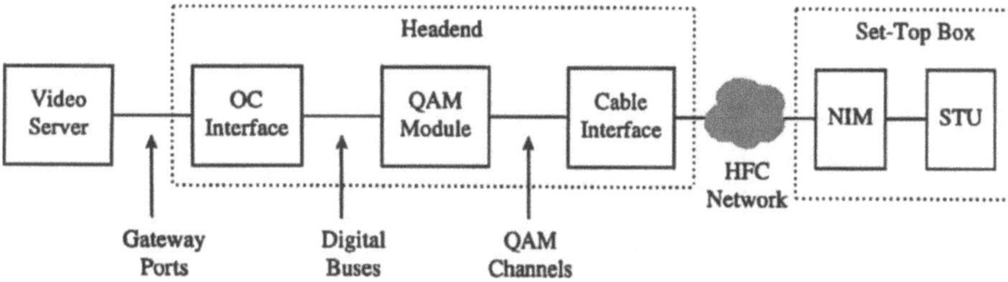

Figure 2. Video delivery flow.

SONET network. The network between video server and headend is a core network and may have ATM switches for switching and routing. The OC module in the headend converts the optical signal to the electric signal and extracts ATM cells from the SONET frame. The ATM cells, then, are sent to the QAM module where the digital signal is modulated to the analog signal in 6 MHz bandwidth. There are 9 QAM modules and 9 QAM channels to the cable module in which each QAM channel is shifted to the appropriate channel and is combined with the analog TV signal with a combiner. The combined signals are then output to the HFC network.

There are two common transport mechanisms for delivering video from a video server to the STB. One mechanism is ATM to the STB structure where ATM cells carrying MPEG-2 video are transported from the video server to STBs without segmentation and reassembly of the video, only the physical layer conversion during the delivery. That is, it converts optical OC-3c SONET frame to the electric signal in the headend and modulates to the RF analog signal and transports over the network. Then, it demodulates to the digital signal in the network interface module of the STB. Another mechanism is MPEG-2 to the STB structure where ATM cells carrying MPEG-2 video terminates at the headend and reassembles the payload of the cells to a 188-byte MPEG-2 TS which is modulated to analog RF signal and transported to the STB over the HFC network. There are advantages and disadvantages of each method. In the MPEG-2 to the STB structure, no SAR (segmentation and reassembly) chip is needed in each Network Interface Module (NIM), thus reducing the STB cost. It also has better bandwidth utilization. However, this structure is only good for video delivery, but not for data or voice services. The ATM to the STB structure has slightly inefficient bandwidth utilization and it needs an SAR chip at each NIM. However, the structure has more flexibility and is suitable for video delivery as well as for data and voice services. The choice of the system depends on the system requirement, cost issue, and the underlying network. For more details, please see [7]. The ATM to the STB is implemented in this trial.

C. Hybrid fiber coax network

In order to investigate the effect of HFC network on the VOD system, the network deployed in the trial is not a simple HFC network which has only a fiber node [10]. Rather, six HFC networks and two signal distribution centers are involved in this trial as depicted in figure 3. The video server and headend equipments are housed in NCHC (National Center

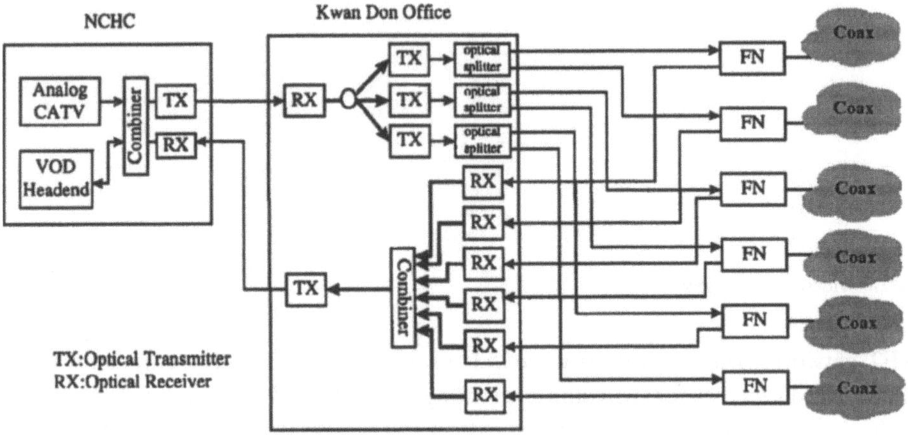

Figure 3. Hybrid fiber coax network in the VOD trial.

for High-Performance Computing, Hsinchu, Taiwan) where analog cable TV signals are also available. A combiner combines all conventional CATV signals and the downstream signal from the VOD headend. The combined signal is fed into the optical transmitter. The optical signal from NCHC is transmitted to the central office in Kwan Don office where the optical signals are received by optical receiver and converted to electrical downstream signals. The downstream signals are split into three signals by a splitter. Then, each signal is converted to the optical signal which is again split into two optical signals by an optical splitter. After performing conversion and splitting in the central office, six same optical signals are sent to six fiber nodes where coax cable networks are deployed. The fiber node has an optical receiver that converts the optical signal back to the downstream signal and sends to the coax network. The coax network has amplifiers, directional couplers, splitters and taps that distribute signals to the customers. There are uninterrupted power supplies in the fiber node to power optical and electrical equipments and to maintain the stability of the power.

In the upstream direction, the control signals are sent from the STB in the upstream channels at the same coax network. There are optical transmitters in the fiber nodes to convert upstream signal into optical signal and transmit them to the central office. The optical signal upstream signal is converted back to the electrical signal and is combined with all other upstream signals. The combined upstream signals go through another optical-electrical conversion. Finally, the upstream signals are sent to the headend.

D. *Content preparation*

If a computer comes without software, it is useless even though it may be a sophisticated machine. Similarly, the VOD system is an engineer's toy from the perspective of the customer if it does not provide excellent programs and rich contents. Hence content plays an important role in the successful deployment of a VOD system. The content provided in this

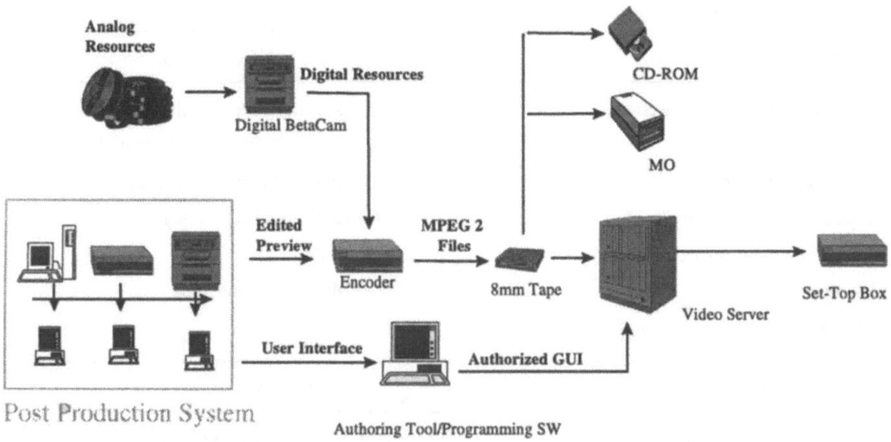

Figure 4. Content preparation flow.

trial is grouped into three categories: Movie-Express, Pop Music and Instant News. These contents are supplied by studios, record companies and domestic cable news networks. The process of content preparation is described in the following. It can be divided into 4 phases which are content creation and capture, content editing, authoring and content loading.

(1) *Content creation and capture.* The content elements are text, video, audio, graphics, animation and etc. These elements may come from different sources—it may come from studios or record companies or be created in house or even by purchasing. If the elements are not in the digital form, they have to be converted to digital form for computer processing. All the elements are loaded into computer.
(2) *Content editing.* The designers use computer software to edit the elements such as color correction, music editing or adding special effects.
(3) *Authoring.* Like a director to direct a movie, the designers need to integrate all the content elements such as video, graphics, captions in a coherent way.
(4) *Content loading.* After the content has been authored, it becomes a complete file which can be saved in a 8 mm tape. The files can be converted to different formats and loaded to the video server as shown in figure 4.

III. System integration

The system integration involves not only a variety of technologies, such as network, communication, computer, video, software, but content and programs. Table 1 lists some of the issues that challenge system designers. Examining these issues will find that the compatibility is the topic that is addressed in most areas. It is no surprise because entities of the system come from various manufacturers and the existing standards do not cover the whole system even though the Digital Audio-Visual Council (DAVIC) attempts to do such

Table 1. System integration issues.

End-to-end system	HFC network
(1) End-to-end network connectivity	(1) Overall network architecture
(2) End-to-end latency	(2) Spectrum allocation fiber node size
(3) L1 gateway functionality	(3) Return channel MAC protocols
(4) L2 gateway functionality	(4) End-to-end signal quality
(5) Management system architecture	(5) Jitter
(6) System security	(6) Modulation schemes
(7) User data collection	

Video server/VDT gateway	Encoder
(1) OC interface compatibility	(1) Large file system to hold video files (>2.7 GB)
(2) AAL /ATM compatibility	(2) Fast file system/network to sustain 3 Mbps traffics
(3) VPI/VCI to QAM channel mapping	(3) Tape format compatibility
(4) Congestion resolution	(4) MPEG content compatibility
(5) L1 gateway compatibility	
(6) L2 gateway compatibility	

NIM/STB	Application development	Content preparation
(1) A0 interface compatibility	(1) Robust OS selection	(1) Content capture
(2) MPEG compatibility	(2) Authoring tools	(2) Format conversion
(3) OS porting	(3) Chinese fonts	(3) Non-linear editing
(4) Chinese fonts engine	(4) Download capability	
	(5) AP development tools	

an ambitious job [4]. The compatibility issue resides in the physical interface between each entity and in the protocols. The syntax and semantics of the controls and commands have to be consistent across the whole system from the encoder to the STBs. Any slight inconsistency will cause the system to hang up. The trial system is built to follow DAVIC specifications as closely as possible. The S1 interface is chosen to carry the primary service, i.e., video. The network interface module (NIM) of STB is partially confirmed to A0 interface of DAVIC.

The Chinese font problem is the severe trouble to be overcome as most application development tools for VOD systems do not provide the character-based Chinese fonts. One way to circumvent the problem is to treat a Chinese character as a bitmap instead of a code, like ASCII code. However, the problem is only partially resolved by doing it this way. For example, a string of texts can be passed as parameters between functions in a program while it is difficult to pass bitmaps as the parameters. A special Chinese font engine needs to be made in order to solve the problem. That means more budget and a longer deployment schedule.

The end-to-end latency of the system is targeted in the range of one to two seconds. We are still in the process of fine tuning the system to meet the goal of 1 second. It has been verified that a user is unaware of the delay if the end-to-end latency is less than 400 ms. However, if the latency is beyond 3 seconds, the user may find the service unsatisfactory. The video server and headend may receive excessive commands when the user impatiently waits for the system to respond and presses the remote controller repetitively. Network delay should be as small as possible compared to the total system allowable latency.

Interactive VOD requires not only a bound on delay but also a bound on the jitters. While latency is inevitably caused by physical media and switching, variation of latency (or statistical distribution of the per-packet communication delay), which is called jitters, is mainly introduced by network. The quality of the service depends on not only MPEG-2 related technologies and fine contents but also the network jitters. The network jitters cause the mosaic in the video display and produce the "firecracker" sound. One way to reduce jitters might be to eliminate the statistical behavior of the network by using buffering. In addition to the buffers used in the server and headend, the NIM in STB equips with a 64 K buffer to reduce the network jitters. It is our goal of designing a special circuitry in the NIM to reduce the buffer size as much as possible because a big size buffer implies a long latency.

Content is not a technical problem that an engineer has to tackle with, yet it determines the success of the VOD trial from the perspective of the general public. To obtain the content sources and to ensure the constant supplies, a content preparation team has been established. The team negotiates with studios, record companies and TV stations to acquire the copyright for public usage. Since it is free to use the VOD system and the CCL can not afford to pay for the royalty, contents are provided free to this trial. Therefore, the movies in the trial probably are not the first run ones. Another issue that is not urgent but a serious concern is "what is next after this trial." The trial is conducted by the CCL which is a research and development lab, not an operational corporation. The project of conducting this trial is finished when it reaches the goal. After that, the system should be handed over to an appropriate organization and should not discontinue services because of project termination. All the issues, technical or non-technical, have to be well prepared before the inauguration of the Video-On-Demand system which is scheduled for June 1997.

The survey of consumers' reaction to all possible aspects of the system is one of the major tasks as planned from the beginning. Since the trial will be conducted till the end of December 1997, final data is not available at this time of writing. However, from a couple of surveys that have been conducted so far we learn that most of the users are in favor of choosing entertainment contents like movies rather than education or training materials. They would prefer to having movies varying from fictions to classics. Evidence shows that people with ages older than 40 are not excited about the concept of interactive uses. On the other hand, younger people tend to be very computer oriented and they are quite excited in having the option to select their favorite movies on their demands. Data reveals that higher picture quality is not as important as generally expected as long as it displays VCR quality. This fact tends to support the argument that contents are more critical than quality.

From this trial, we have obtained experiences from components to the end-to-end system integration. Lacking of well proven standards and architectures, different vendors' co-operation and interfaces between different modules were proved to be difficult tasks of the trial. With few selections available, we were forced to make the compromise on the system specification. For instance, we did not have many choices of picking a mature (well developed and tested with good support) real time OS designed for the task of VOD. A bug in the OS caused the delay of the project for months.

IV. Conclusion

Once the VOD system becomes operational, it can meet the needs from different industries. Local computer and cable equipment manufacturers can test their products such as video servers, STBs, network equipment on the testbed. Multiple Services Operators (MSO) can deploy new interactive services such as Near-VOD, VOD, home shopping and Internet access. Software developers can integrate various interactive multimedia applications to the testbed. Although the current trial system supports 200 customers, the system is by no means restricted to it. The system will grow as more video severs and STBs add in. The competition between state-run organizations and private business heats up as telecommunication deregulation is underway in Taiwan where the home pass rate of the cable network has reached 80%. An interactive multimedia industry is emerging. Lessons learned from deploying the VOD system can dictate a migration path to the full service network development.

Acknowledgment

The authors are indebted to the following people who provided valuable information and comments for this article: Wen-Chen Pang, Hsin-Yun Wu, Theresa Hou of CCL/ ITRI, and Brian Chen of Integrated Network Corporation.

Note

1. The research of this paper is supported as part of the project 3HU1K01 FY85 sponsored by the Ministry of Economic Affairs (MOEA), Taiwan, ROC. The views and conclusions contained in this document are those of authors and should not be interpreted as representing the official policies of MOEA.

References

1. C. Blank, "The FSN challenge: Large-scale interactive television," IEEE Computer, Vol. 28, Vo. 5, pp. 9–12, May 1995.
2. R.W. Brown and J.W. Callahan, "Software architecture for broadband CATV interactive systems," 1995 NCTA Technical Papers, pp. 270–278.
3. Y.-H. Chang, D. Coggins, D. Pitt, D. Skellern, M. Thapar, and C. Venkatraman, "An open-system approach to video on demand," IEEE Commun. Magazine, Vol. 32. No. 5, pp. 68–80, May 1994.
4. DAVIC, "DAVIC 1.0 specification," 1996.
5. J.-J. Hsue, "Video-On-Demand (VOD) system specifications," Technical Reference No. 113850166, CCL/ITRI.
6. J.-J. Hsue, C.-W. Cheng, J.-L. Liu, K.-J. Chou, and C.-I. Wang, "VOD system design issues (in Chinese)," CCL Technical Journal, Vol. 43, pp. 3–11, Oct. 1995.

7. T. Kwok, "A vision for residential broadband services: ATM-to-the-home," IEEE Network, Vol. 9, No. 5, pp. 14–28, Sept./Oct. 1995.
8. V. Loen and E. Miller, "Subscriber terminal units for video dial tone systems," IEEE Network, Vol. 9, No. 5, pp. 48–57, Sept./Oct. 1995.
9. T.S. Perry, "The trials and travails of interactive TV," IEEE Spectrum, pp. 22–28, April 1996.
10. W. Pugh and G. Boyer, "Broadband access: Comparing alternatives," IEEE Commun. Magazine, Vol. 33, No. 8, pp. 34–46, Aug. 1995.
11. M.P. Vecchi, "Broadband networks and services: Architecture and control," IEEE Commun. Magazine, Vol. 33. No. 8, pp. 24–32, Aug. 1995.

Dr. Yuan Liang Su received his Ph.D. in System Engineering from Georgia Institute of Technology in 1985. He was an Associate Professor of the Department of Computer Science at National Taiwan University, Taiwan from 1985 to 1986. He joined Bell Labs and participated in the early planning and development of the Intelligent Network from 1986 to 1991. He became an Associate Professor of the Department of Industrial Engineering & Management at National Chiao Tung University, Taiwan in 1991. He is currently the Deputy General Director of the Computer & Communication Research Labs, Industrial Technology Research Institute, Taiwan. He is now responsible for the Communication R&D activities including: Network Management, Broadband Services, PCS/IN, Access Technologies etc.

Dr. Kae-Jy Chou received his M.S.E.E. from the Polytechnic University in 1985 and Ph.D. in Electrical Engineering from the University of Michigan in 1993. Form 1985 to 1988, he worked as project engineer for the Superior Manufacturing Inc. From 1993 to 1995, he worked for American System Technology Inc. Now, he works as staff engineer for the Computer & Communication Research Labs, Industrial Technology Research Institute, Taiwan. His current research interests include network planning, protocol design and system integration.

Dr. Chih-Wen Cheng received his Ph.D. in Applied Mathematics from Carnegie Mellon University in 1993 with speciality in optimal control. He currently works for Computer & Communication Laboratories (CCL) of Industrial Technology Research Institute (ITRI) as the K320 Session Manager of Broadband Network Systems Department (K300). He is expert & interested in the research of Video Systems, Object-oriented Design, Multimedia & Hypermedia Systems, Symbolic Calculation, Control and Optimization, and Calculus of Variations. He is one of the representatives of CCL to DAVIC (Digital Audio Visual Council) international standard meeting. He has many papers published by like Archive for Rational Mechanics and Analysis, SIAM Journal of Control and Optimization, and IEEE Conference On Decision and Control etc.

Dr. Jin-Jen Hsue received his M.S. and Ph.D. both in Electrical Engineering from the University of Michigan in 1993. Form 1993 to 1996, he worked as staff engineer for the Computer & Communication Research Labs, Industrial Technology Research Institute, Taiwan. He is currently a session manager and responsible for broadband system integration.

Dr. Fuyung Lai received his Ph.D. in Electrical and Computer Engineering from North Carolina State University in 1990. He was an advising engineer/scientist in IBM Research Triangle Park and participated in the research area of Frame Relay, ATM, and Interactive Multi-media Communication systems. He is currently the Manager of Broadband Network Systems Department of the Computer & Communication Research Lab's., Industrial

Technology Research Institute, Taiwan. He is now involved in the activities of Interactive Multi-media Networking Systems, Broadband Services, and Broadband Access Technologies.

Dr. Jun-Lin Liu received a B.S. in computer science from Tamkang University, and the M.S. and Ph.D. from the University of Missouri, Rolla, in 1984, 1989 and 1993, respectively. He is currently a staff engineer in the Computer & Communication Research Labs, Industrial Technology Research Institute, Taiwan. He is currently on the NII video-on-demand project. His research interests include parallel processing, multimedia system and high speed networks.

Chun-I Wang received a B.S. in Electrical Engineering from Nation Taiwan University, and the M.S.E.E. from the University of Florida in 1988 and 1993, respectively. From 1993 to 1994, he was a System Analyst of the Institute for Simulation and Training of University of Central Florida. Form 1995, he works as an Associate Engineer for the Computer & Communication Research Labs, Industrial Technology Research Institute, Taiwan. His current research interest include multimedia, Internet protocols, high speed serial bus and video on demand system integration.

Multimedia Tools and Applications 5, 199–205 (1997)

"NTT's Joint Utilization Tests of Multimedia Communications"—Utilization Tests for CATV and VOD over FTTH

ISAO OMIYA omiya@mod.hqs.ntt.co.jp
Network Services Department, Nippon Telegraph and Telephone Corporation (NTT), 3-20-2 Nishi-shinjuku, Shinjuku-ku, Tokyo 163-14, Japan

Abstract. NTT is carrying out "Utilization Tests for CATV Video Transmissions" that provide CATV video transmissions, Video-on-demand (VOD) and ISDN services on an integrated basis to participating subscribers. In these tests, optical fibers are installed under the Fiber-to-the-Home (FTTH) concept in three trial areas, each having about 300 subscribers, and two types of transmission systems are used: FDM-PON and ATM-PON. The trial is scheduled to finish at the end of March, 1997.

Keywords: VOD, Passive Optical Network (PON), Fiber-to-the-Home (FTTH), CATV

1. Introduction

Since 1988, NTT has been providing analog Video on Demand Service (analog image storage, analog transmission) to special groups such as the fashion industry, a local government, and a museum.

However, advances in digital image processing technology and computer technology have greatly raised general users' interest in multimedia.

At the same time, telecommunications technology has been making a transition from analog systems to digital/ATM systems and from metallic wiring to optical fiber, all of which is bringing us closer to the multimedia communication era. NTT has already introduced optical fibers under the Fiber-to-the Office (FTTO) or the Fiber-to-the-Zone (FTTZ) concepts, but to support multimedia communications, the Fiber-to-the-Home (FTTH) concept is very important.

It was under these circumstances that NTT decided to carry out a field trial (Utilization Tests for CATV Video Transmissions) focusing on CATV, VOD, and ISDN services and applications of the FTTH generation from September 1995 to March 1997. Three types of VOD systems, each consisting of servers and set–top boxes (STBs) and two types of transmission systems (FDM-PON and ATM-PON) have been installed at three sites.

This paper describes the trial, transmission systems, and VOD systems.

2. Utilization tests for CATV video transmissions

This trial, called "Utilization Tests for CATV Video Transmissions", has the following objectives:

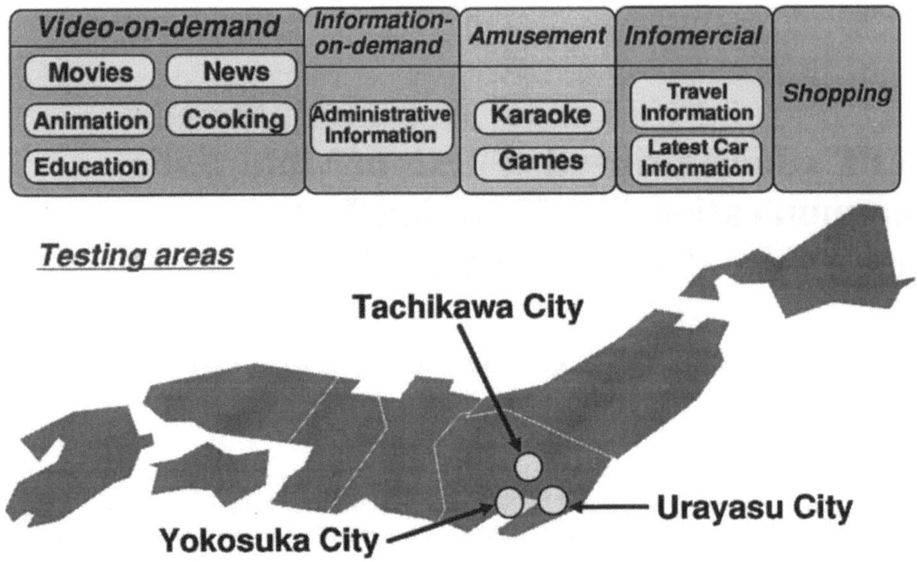

Figure 1. Utilization tests for CATV video transmissions.

— Evaluate new subscriber network technology.
— Estimate the profitability of various subscriber systems and applications.
— Develop new interactive services that can be offered by content and service providers.
— Examine the feasibility of business-oriented applications.

The trial is being carried out as a joint-project by CATV operators, content providers, and NTT as a telecom operator. NTT provides the network system, related equipment, and software between CATV headend and subscribers homes. The CATV operators provide the interactive services such as CATV and VOD and the content providers provide contents for these systems and services. During the course of the trial, we have been carrying out surveys to consider the commercial feasibility of the services and technologies.

The systems have been installed in three trial sites near Tokyo (Tachikawa, Urayasu, and Yokosuka), and the services are being provided to about 300 subscribers from among 10,000 CATV subscribers in each area. The overview of the trial is shown in figure 1.

Two transmission systems based on the FTTH concept have been developed for the trial. One is a Frequency Division Multiplexing-Passive Optical Network (FDM-PON) and the other is an Asynchronous Transmission Mode-Passive Optical Network (ATM-PON). By using both systems in this trial, we can evaluate which services and applications are more suitable for each system.

Each VOD system can store about 200 hours of moving pictures that can be distributed to 100 terminals simultaneously. The images are encoded in an MPEG2 format and sounds are encoded in an MPEG1 audio format. Each system has a different human-machine interface.

The information is being provided from content providers and consists mainly of movies, animation, news, community information, karaoke music, video games, and travel guides. Some of this information, such as movies, is provided as pay programs.

3. Transmission systems

In this trial, the basic network topology of the transmission system is point-to-multipoint passive double star. However, star is actually the topology between an NTT office and subscriber homes because optical couplers are installed in NTT offices. The reason for this is that the current optical fiber test system is designed for a point-to-point configuration and cannot operate under a point-to-multipoint configuration.

The above topology has some advantages, such as:

— Simplified management and maintenance of the optical fiber core and coupler and,
— Ease of combining current services such as telephone service with video transmission.

This topology uses couplers which split the optical signal directly, so that the split optical signal energy is weakened. This means that the maximum transmission distance and the signal-to-noise ratio of this system depend on the number of coupler splits.

The signal multiplexing of telephone and video is carried out by a technology called Wavelength Division Multiplexing (WDM). An optical device called a Wavelength Division Multiplexer combines two optical signals of different wavelengths into one optical fiber core on the sending side and separates them on the receiving side.

The transmission systems used in this trial are an FDM-PON system based on FDM technology and an ATM-PON system based on ATM technology.

3.1. FDM-PON system

The configuration of the FDM-PON system is shown in figure 2. The system consists of transmission equipment (FM-TA/RA, AM-TA/RA, etc.) installed in both an NTT office and

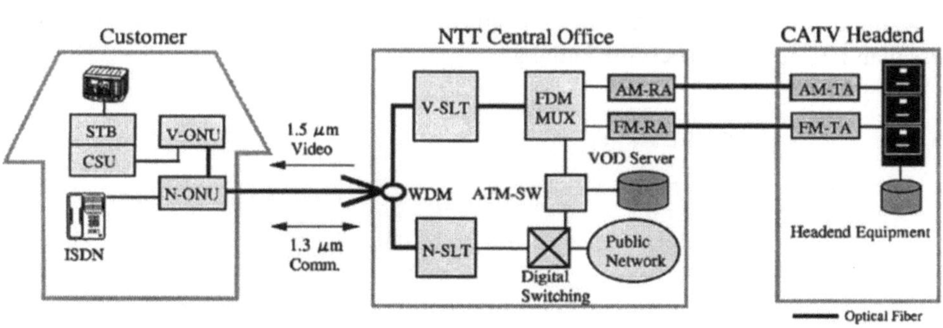

Figure 2. FDM-PON system configuration.

a CATV operator's office to transmit video signals from the CATV operator, a FDM multiplexer (FDM-MUX), a video subscriber line terminal (V-SLT), a narrowband subscriber line terminal (N-SLT), and an ordinary digital switching system installed in a NTT office, and a video optical network unit (V-ONU), a narrowband optical network unit (N-ONU), and set-top box (STB) installed in the subscribers' home.

Narrowband signals such as those for telephone are processed as an ISDN signal (BRI) and transmitted by time compression multiplexing (TCM) using a 1.3 μm wavelength optical signal between a N-SLT and a N-ONU. The N-ONU terminates the optical signal from the N-SLT and converts it into an electrical signal before providing it to a digital terminal. The N-ONU also separates a 1.5 μm optical signal that includes a video signal from the wavelength multiplexed signal. An ISDN port is installed in the N-ONU and one of the B channels is used for the uplink to control VOD.

While guaranteeing sufficient transmission distance and signal-to- noise ratio of the video signal for all subscribers in the field, the input signal is branched into eight signals in this system. To ensure a communication channel for each terminal, Time Division Multiplexing (TDM) was adopted for the downlink and Time Division Multiple Access (TDMA) for the uplink to assign the necessary time slots.

The video signal is transmitted by a 1.3 μm wavelength optical signal. Eleven basic (terrestrial broadcast) channels received at a CATV operator's office are transmitted to an NTT office in the FDM-AM (Amplitude Modulation) format as they are. Thirty-six channels, including programs received from BS/CS (Broadcast Satellite/Communication Satellite), and original programs are multiplexed in a FDM-FM (Frequency Modulation) format and transmitted to the NTT office. The frequency assignment is shown in figure 3. The VOD video signal, which is an MPEG2 encoded digital signal, is combined with the CATV signal by quadrature amplitude modulation (QAM) and frequency multiplexing. VOD differs from CATV in that the latter transmits the same signal to all subscribers who individually select which signal to view on their side.

In VOD, however, the server must select and send the program requested from a subscriber's STB and the subscriber must pick it up from the designated channel. For this reason, the VOD system must be able to multiplex more channels to provide VOD services to multiple subscribers simultaneously. Multiplexing more channels, however, requires that a high Carrier Noise Ratio (CNR) be maintained. We therefore adopted the 16 QAM for this trial.

The quality of the video signal is as the same as that of satellite broadcasting services. In addition, the CNR of the AM signal is greater than 48 dB, and the error rate of QAM is less than 10^{-11}, which meets the initial goal.

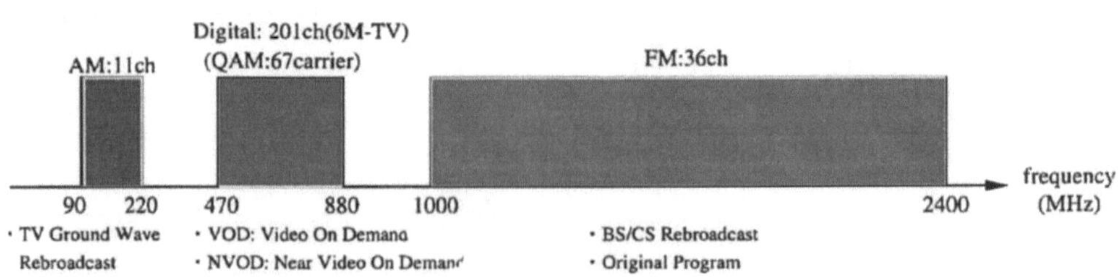

Figure 3. Frequency allocation.

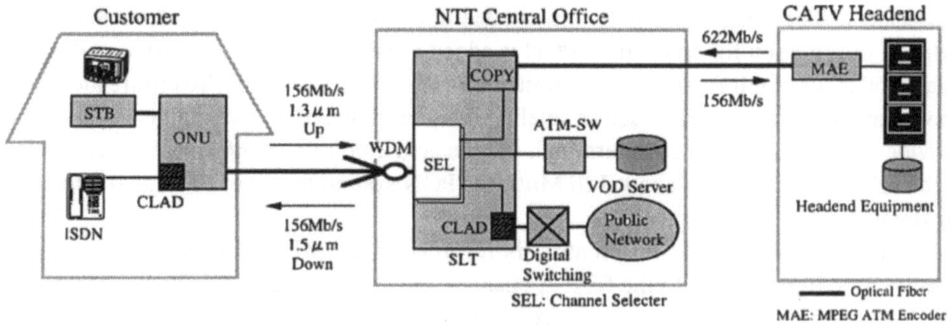

Figure 4. ATM-PON system configuration.

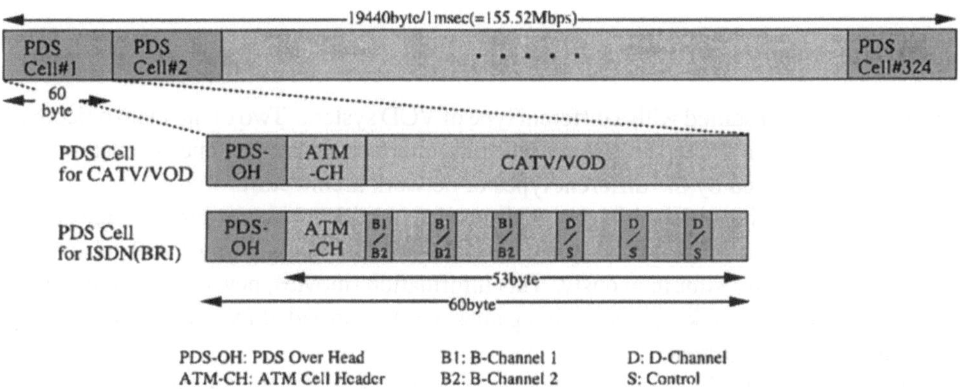

Figure 5. ATM frame format.

3.2. *ATM-PON system*

The configuration of the ATM-PON system is shown in figure 4. The system consists of an SLT, an ATM switch, and an ordinal switching system installed in an NTT office, a Real-time MPEG-ATM Encoder in the CATV operator's office, and an ONU and a STB installed in subscribers' homes.

A 1.3 μm optical signal for the uplink and a 1.5 μm optical signal for the downlink are multiplexed by WDM and transmitted at a bit rate of 156 Mb/s. To avoid signal collision in the uplink, the signal is controlled by TDMA because subscriber lines are formed in a passive double star configuration.

The telephone signal is provided as an ISDN signal and multiplexed by the video signal. The B and D channels of ISDN are assigned to ATM cells by the Partial Filling Method. The frame format of this system is shown in figure 5.

The CATV image signal, which is composed of dozens of programs, is encoded immediately into MPEG2 format by the Real-time MPEG-ATM Encoder and transformed into ATM cells at a bit rate of 622 Mb/s. Because of the bit-rate limitation (about 150 Mb/s) of a subscriber line, only the signal of the channel selected at a terminal is transmitted to subscribers. The image information is divided into 53-byte ATM cells. Moreover, seven bytes of information for controlling PON is added as an overhead to each ATM cell, and a total of 60 bytes of information is transmitted to a subscriber as one cell. To ensure the whole service and the video quality such as satellite broadcasting in this system, it is necessary to provide 15 Mb/s signal to each terminal. As the actual bit rate of information transmitted at the subscriber section is about 120 Mb/s, the PON system branches the signal into eight bit streams.

In the VOD system, the information is recorded in an MPEG2 format and provided directly as a digital signal to the SLT. A channel selector in the SLT selects the channel or VOD program in accordance with the request from a terminal. In general, the time delay resulting from the channel selection process is annoying to viewers, but about 0.5 seconds of this system time delay is almost the same as that of ordinary operations with an STB of a CATV system, which is not especially annoying.

4. VOD system

Each site has been installed with a different type of VOD system. Two of the main objectives of this trial are to evaluate the human-machine interface or service and to examine the conformance achieved by the different types of network architecture.

Up to about 200 hours of the image signal encoded in MPEG2 format and the audio signal encoded in MPEG1 format can be stored in each server. A maximum of 100 subscribers can access each server simultaneously. This information (movies, news, community information, animation, karaoke music, video games, etc.) is provided by content providers as programs in a digital format.

The VOD system for FDM-PON system is using an ISDN dial-up line (single B channel) as the uplink and has a unit which concentrates the control signal through a digital switching system. The VOD system for the ATM-PON system, however, directly transmits the control signal in the ATM format.

The server is composed of a Management Server that stores menu information and subscriber information, a Video Server that stores video information, and an Application Server that stores still picture images and the control information for retrieving. The ATM switch connects the servers and terminal channels in accordance with requests from terminals for programs, which users select according to a menu displayed on the TV screen, and transfers the information data as a 6 Mb/s bit stream.

The VOD systems do not meet the recommended specifications issued by the Digital Audio Visual Council (DAVIC) because the systems were developed before the specifications were issued.

5. Conclusion

Since the start of the field trial in September 1995, the systems have been operating successfully. Although we cannot provide a comprehensive analysis of all the systems because the trial continued until the end of March 1997, we can offer the following preliminary report.

The FDM-PON and ATM-PON transmission systems have achieved stable operation, and the video quality of the transmission systems and the VOD systems has met our target.

Access traffic has increased as users have become more experienced. The access frequency of each program, user satisfaction, and feasibility issues, etc., are being measured but need to be carefully analyzed as they depend on users' tastes and needs.

The systems have so far proven to be technically feasible for commercial use. In future they will be improved to make them more economical for commercial implementation.

References

1. K. Harikae, K. Yoshimura, N. Miki, and H. Yoshinaga, "Optical access systems for narrowband communication and video distribution," NTT R&D, Vol. 44, No. 12, pp. 1157–1162, 1995.
2. T. Kanada and N. Terada, "ATM-PDS-based broadband fiber access system," NTT R&D, Vol. 44, No. 12, pp. 1163–1170, 1995.
3. I. Sakakibara and Y. Motohashi, "Trial of CATV, VOD and ISDN services over FTTH," IEEE 3rd International Workshop on Community Networking, pp. 33–38, 1996.

Isao Omiya after receiving a B.E. in 1980 and M.E. in 1982 from Shizuoka University, Japan, Isao Omiya entered Nippon Telegraph and Telephone Corporation (NTT) in 1982. He has worked in developing Digital Data Networks and Video Response System (Analog VOD) and in planning deployment of fiber optic subscriber lines in local areas. He is currently a Senior Manager in the Network Service Department of NTT and is in charge of developing new services based on optical fiber. From 1985 to 1986 he studied at the Institute Nationale Polytechnique de Grenoble (INPG), France. He is a member of The Institute of Electronics, Information and Communication Engineers.

Multimedia Tools and Applications 5, 207–216 (1997)

Interactive Television Trials and Marketplace Experiences

JOHN CAREY JTCAREY@aol.com
Greystone Communications, 17, Bellair Drive, Dobbs Ferry, NY 10522

Abstract. This article provides a review of ITV trials and services from the 1970s through the mid 1990s. It presents an annotated history of ITV and draws a number of lessons about content, pricing, consumer appeal and advertising within an interactive television context. ITV has alternated between peaks of marketing hyperbole and valleys of skepticism. A realistic path of development may now be emerging.

Keywords: interactive TV; video-on-demand; consumer adoption

It is often assumed that interactive television (ITV) is a relatively new, untested phenomenon. Under these conditions, only speculation is possible about how consumers will respond to ITV when it is made available at some point in the future. In reality, there is a considerable body of knowledge and experience about ITV and consumer responses to it. This knowledge and experience can inform decisions about the development of new interactive television services.

What is interactive TV?

What is interactive television? There are many perspectives. These include much greater selection of programming on hundreds of channels, more control over TV viewing, customization of television programming, on-demand delivery of video programs and movies, and real time interaction between people in different households via game playing. Some argue that ITV must include video; others believe that interactive text displayed on a TV set also qualifies as ITV.

There is no consensus on what interactive television means or what it includes. Given the many differing perspectives, it may be premature to try to define interactive television. Time and the marketplace will likely sort out the definitional problem. In place of an accepted definition for ITV, it may be more useful to outline a spectrum or grid of characteristics and then to classify different systems by the number and types of characteristics they meet.

There is also disagreement about the core technology(ies) that will provide a base for interactive television. This involves not only the many complex issues associated with the network architecture for transmitting ITV but even the basic question of what the household terminal will be. Many believe that the household terminal will be a standard television set; others believe that a personal computer will serve as the host technology in homes; and still others are placing their bets on videogame players as the ITV terminal.

In trying to come to grips with the potential and the reality of ITV, it is useful to step back and review the history of interactive television. What has been learned from earlier ITV efforts and what lessons can be applied today? In the review that follows, the definition of ITV is broad. It includes some interactive text systems that used regular television sets as the display terminal, video telephones, and some institutional applications for two-way video. However, it does not include trials and services of interactive video accessed via personal computers, interactive formats within regular television programs or video telephones [17].

A history of interactive TV from the 1970s to the 1990s

During the 1970s, there were many trials and tests for interactive television. The National Science Foundation sponsored three major trials utilizing interactive cable television for education, community services and worker training [21]; the U.S. Department of Health, Education and Welfare (DHEW) supported a number of tests and services utilizing interactive television for health care; and a large commercial test of interactive cable TV (Warner Amex's Qube system in Columbus, Ohio) received considerable publicity. It is difficult to summarize the results of these tests and services succinctly. However, a few lessons can be drawn. First, there were many technical problems. Equipment was often in a prototype stage of development and it was not consistently reliable. This had a negative impact on many tests. Second, equipment was generally expensive. Often, the user group could not afford the equipment without the aid of a federal or foundation sponsor. Third, there were many organizational problems associated with implementation of the service that had little to do with the interactive technology as such. Some organizations forgot that technological innovations are also social innovations. They require changes in behavior and often meet resistance by those with entrenched habits. Nonetheless, many needed and wanted services did emerge. They were adopted directly by organizations and communities or evolved into permanent services. In this sense, the results of these trials and tests were mixed, not a dismal failure as is sometimes attributed to them.

Qube deserves special mention since it is cited frequently as an example of failed interactive technology. Qube technology was very expensive, particularly in a 1970s context. The Qube terminal in homes cost approximately $200, or, four times the cost of standard decoders at that time, and Qube equipment at the cable headend added approximately $2–3 million in plant costs. In addition, it was expensive and difficult to maintain the upstream or return data path from homes. This introduced reliability problems for the interactive service.

Production costs and interactive program design presented further obstacles. Budgets for Qube programs were very low compared to broadcast network programming budgets. "Interactivity" with low production values could not compete with network programming. Moreover, those producing interactive programs were starting from scratch: there was little previous experience in designing interactive programs.

While many households subscribed to Qube, actual use of Qube programming was generally low. However, there were a few exceptions. Some game format programs achieved moderate viewership and strong interactive participation from those watching. Qube also demonstrated that pay-per-view programming was potentially viable—if the cost of promoting and processing pay-per-view orders could be reduced. And, Qube introduced a number of interactive formats that have since evolved and been adopted as components in cable and broadcast programming. In this sense, Qube was an important programming laboratory—MTV and Nickelodeon both trace their roots to Qube programming.

Cost of the technology, low production values and problems in maintaining the upstream data path were sufficient to doom Qube in a late 1970s—early 1980s context. In addition, Qube had served as a franchising tool for Warner Amex: the promise of interactive programming helped them to win many franchises. After the franchising wars of the early 1980s were completed, the marketing value of Qube for Warner Amex was eliminated.

During the 1980s in the U.S., there was a movement away from high-end ITV services like Qube and towards simpler services like interactive text on TV, interactive games over cable and opinion polling during regular TV programs via special 900 number telephone services . Many of these services were videotex precursors to online services for the personal computer. However, in the early and mid 1980s, the television set remained prominent as a display device since relatively few households had a personal computer.

In the cable environment, Cox Cable developed a service in the early 1980s, Indax, that was intended to compete with Qube as a franchising tool. Indax was really a videotex service over two-way cable. It offered home banking, shopping, information services and education content but it contained no video—only text and simple graphics. Indax was tested in Omaha and San Diego but never entered the broad marketplace. During this same period, Time Inc. developed Time Teletext and tested it in Orlando and San Diego. Time Teletext was a one-way teletext service but since it used an entire cable channel, it could transmit a few thousand frames in several seconds and simulate interactivity, e.g., for games and quizzes. Time Teletext experienced the same fate as Indax. It was withdrawn after field testing. In both cases, the cost of the technology was very high and the marketplace response was lukewarm. For example, Time Teletext required a special decoder that cost over $500 and a large staff to update content. Users indicated that they liked Time Teletext but would pay only $5–7 per month for both the service and the box [14]. In this sense, Time Teletext was an attractive service for many consumers but it was not a viable business.

During the 1980s, many specialized cable channels were created but there was relatively little space available on the existing cable systems. Two of the new channels offered interactive games: Play Cable and Nabu Network. Neither succeeded in gaining space on large numbers of cable systems. Further, they did not receive sufficient market exposure to determine if consumers really wanted them.

QUBE, Time Teletext, Indax and other commercial services received a great deal of attention in the popular press during the 1980s. Meanwhile, a large set of very simple interactive television services was emerging quietly in education. In a few cases, the services utilized full two-way video between teachers and students who were at a distance. However, in most instances the model involved one-way video instruction via satellite, cable or ITFS (Instructional Television Fixed Service, a microwave frequency) with return audio via a regular telephone call. Later, electronic mail, fax and dedicated data terminals were added as return paths to the instructor. These services reached thousands of students in the 1980s at primary, secondary and university levels. Typically, they provided courses that would not otherwise be available in rural areas or small school districts, e.g., Russian and Japanese language courses and advanced mathematics. The Satellite Educational Resources

Consortium, Public Broadcasting Service, National Technology University and several state education networks were among the groups that developed these services in the U.S.

Outside the U.S., there were a number of interactive television projects during the 1980s. Two notable projects were Hi Ovis in Japan [15] and the Biarritz project [6] in France. Both were quite similar in design and findings. They started in the late 1970s and continued through the 1980s, using fiber optic cable to provide video phone calls, interactive text services, better TV reception and extra cable channels, including movies. In both instances, the strong appeal of the services was in providing better TV reception and extra cable channels; the videophones and other interactive services received low usage. However, in both cases much more effort and financial resources went into the development of the technology than in developing interactive programming. The projects were highly visible showcases for advanced technologies that each country was developing.

During 1992–1994 there were a number of interactive television trials and a few actual services in the marketplace. Most utilized a limited form of ITV or provided a limited array of services. Nonetheless, their experiences are informative.

AT&T and Bell Atlantic conducted interactive television trials with groups of employees (AT&T in Chicago and Bell Atlantic in a Virginia surburb of Washington D.C.) to gain experience in operating ITV networks and to get feedback about the attractiveness of services. Both indicated that reactions to the services were positive, while acknowledging that these were preliminary dress rehearsals for larger trials ahead. AT&T reported strong interest by trial homes in interactive educational programs for children, sports, and games where households competed against each other [11]. TCI, AT&T and US West conducted a trial of movies-on-demand in Denver. The 300 test homes purchased 2.5 movies per month, much higher than the national average of 0.26 for pay-per-view homes. However, many homes dropped pay services such as HBO to pay for the movies-on-demand [3]. This may be significant. It appears that people did not increase entertainment spending for interactive services. Rather, they moved spending from one category of the household's entertainment budget to another.

Bell Atlantic reported similar positive results from a large consumer test of its Stargazer video-on-demand service. During a six-month trial in 1,000 homes, the buy rate was 3.3 movies per month. Here too, it appears that consumers shifted money within the household entertainment budget. In this case, they shifted money from video rentals to video-on-demand [16].

A video-on-demand trial in Japan achieved similar results: a buy rate of 3.5 movies per month. However, a different set of conclusions was drawn from the data. This buy rate was judged too low to support the cost of providing video-on-demand infrastructure to homes [10].

A trial by GTE in Cerritos, California appears to have been less successful. Their test service, Main Street, consisted of still video images and sound organized like a database with little updating. Services included access to the Mobil Travel Guide, Grolier's Encyclopedia, Money Manager software and other content that changed little day to day. Overall usage of Main Street was reported to have been low [12]. However, the project generated some useful research findings. GTE found that movies-on-demand were very attractive but consumers were willing to pay only a small increment ($1 extra) for a movie-on-demand over what they paid to rent a movie at a videocassette shop. Further, consumers balked at paying hundreds of dollars for an ITV set-top box and indicated that they would prefer to pay a small rental fee that is part of their cable bill [4].

Two interactive television services were introduced into the marketplace during the early 1990s: Interactive Network (in California and Illinois); and Videoway (in Montreal and Quebec City). Interactive Network required a special terminal costing a few hundred dollars. It also had high monthly charges and the interaction took place not on the TV screen but on a small display attached to the terminal. Services consisted of playing along with TV game shows and trying to anticipate the next play in sporting events. It utilized a multiple choice format and there was no original content. The number of subscribers was modest but this group was reported to be quite enthusiastic about the service. Interactive Network struggled to increase its subscriber base but its death knell came not from subscribers but marketing agreements that brought onboard new company overseers who decided to pull the plug on the service rather than support new marketing efforts [19].

Videoway has no hardware costs for the consumer and a low monthly fee (under $10). Interaction takes place on the TV screen and there is much original content, including daily interactive news programming, games, interactive ads and original programming for children. The service utilizes four channels on the cable system. Much of the interaction takes place by switching from one channel to another where different program components are located. For example, Videoway allows users to choose from four camera angles during coverage of sporting events. Each camera is located on a different channel. They have developed a large subscriber base of more than 230,000 households or more than 20 percent of cable households in the markets where Videoway is available. Usage of Videoway has been reported to be high: subscribing households use the service for 13 hours per week. Approximately half the usage is for games and half for interactive programming [18]. The Videoway service has also been implemented in the United Kingdom. A similar service, developed by ACTV, has been tested in California and is expected to rollout in the U.S. during 1997.

A large number of interactive television trials were announced for both cable and telephone environments in the 1994–1996 time frame. These involved a broad range of cable, telephone and computer companies and many different strategies for delivering services. A half dozen interactive cable TV trials were announced including AT&T and Viacom in Castro Valley; SW Bell and Cox Enterprises in Omaha;, IBM, Videotron and Hearst in Quebec; and Time Warner in Orlando. All of these trials were either cut back sharply from their original plans or cancelled. At the same time, more than 30 major tests of interactive television in a telephone environment were announced, including Ameritech in Chicago; Bell South in North Carolina; GTE in Virginia; US West in Omaha; and SNET in Connecticut. Similarly, each of these trials was either cut back sharply or cancelled.

What happened? It appears that many groups were caught up in a frenzy of trying to corner the interactive television market. They did not carefully examine cost issues. These included very expensive set-top boxes that ranged between $2,000 and $5,000 for the planned trials [5] and the high cost per household to develop the infrastructure for the trials in a mid 1990s time frame. Costs for original interactive content were equally high and none existed.

Time Warner stood alone in offering a high-end interactive TV service with shopping, news, and games as well as video-on-demand in its Full Service Network trial in Orlando.

In the trial with 4,000 test homes, users have been able to order-on-demand from a list of over 100 movies and have the same control over the movies as provided by a VCR, e.g., pause, rewind and fast forward. They have also been able to choose from a group of news stories and watch only those which they want to view. In addition, households can play games against other households. However, Time Warner pulled back from a more ambitious set of service offerings that was announced earlier and has cancelled plans to rollout the service in other markets [13].

As a more realistic picture of costs and technological requirements for ITV emerged, a new strategy was born: evolution. Under this strategy, both cable and telephone companies would develop simpler services with less costly technology and wait for the necessary infrastructure upgrading to take place. This might occur through the natural process of replacing old plant with new equipment or through an accelerated process that would be paid for by demand for other services such as high speed data applications.

There have been many variations on the evolutionary strategy. Some telephone companies decided to develop POCS (Plain Old Cable Service) first, then add interactive services. A number of other telephone companies began to explore so-called wireless cable or ADSL (Asymmetrical Digital Subscriber Line) as relatively inexpensive ways to enter the television service market, while waiting for their telephone plant to be upgraded at a more realistic pace.

In the cable environment, many companies decided to offer Internet services through cable modems and evolve over time to interactive video. Others have begun to offer interactive program guides and other low-end interactive services such as still frame interactive content similar to GTE's Main Street, e.g., UBI in Quebec Province, Canada. A few cable companies, in addition to Time Warner, have conducted trials of movies-on-demand and video programs on-demand. However, the current planning atmosphere is more conservative than a few years earlier.

In Europe, many companies watched the withdrawal of high-end interactive television trials in the U.S. and moved to implement more cost-effective ITV trials, principally offering video-on-demand. British Telecommunications conducted a robust 2,000-home trial with movies-on-demand, home shopping, electronic banking and games in Ipswich and Colchester during 1995–1996. The results were sufficiently positive to encourage them to move forward with an ITV service in London, using British Telecommunications' Westminster cable company. ITV trials have also been conducted in Sweden by Telia AB and in Italy by Telecom Italia. Telia announced a much larger trial for 1997 and plans to deliver interactive multimedia services to nearly all of Sweden by 2004 [20]. In Germany, Deutsche Telekom AG pulled back from its plan for a large scale 4,000-home ITV trial and replaced it with a smaller test of 50 homes in Berlin, to be followed by a modest scale trial in Stuttgart. France Telecom, which conducted an ITV trial in Biaritz during the 1980s, has adopted a conservative wait-and-see attitude. At the same time, France Telecom has conducted a modest 200-home ITV trial in Paris.

The approach to ITV in Europe parallels efforts by cable and telephone companies in the U.S. Companies have been exploiting the existing telecommunications infrastructure, with modest upgrades, to support video-on-demand and other forms of ITV that do not require very expensive home terminals or major network overhauls. As the telecommunication, cable and satellite networks are upgraded over time, they will consider higher-end ITV services.

Discussion

This body of experiences with ITV provides some clues about what consumers want from interactive television, what they are willing to pay, and how services may evolve over time.

Killer applications

There has been much discussion about potential "killer applications"—services or content that will be very attractive to consumers and will drive interactive television into millions of homes. Movies-on-demand and interactive games are two candidate killer applications. However, it may be the case that there are no killer applications and that a critical mass of services will be required to attract large numbers of households. In the ITV trials and services to date, there have been no clear killer applications.

Historically, some media have benefited from so-called killer applications (e.g., HBO helped cable grow during the great expansion period of the 1970s) while other media have required a critical mass of titles or applications (e.g., compact disc players and VCRs).

One ITV analyst, Vincent Grosso, has argued that the search for killer applications is misplaced [9]. In reporting about an ITV trial he supervised for AT&T in Chicago, Grosso indicated that four content attributes were identified: information, gaming, transactions and communication. Each content category such as news or shopping contained one or more of these attributes. For example, sports content contained information (sports scores), gaming (a fantasy baseball game) and communication (opinion boards about sports teams). Consistently throughout the trial, usage increased when additional attributes were added to a content category, e.g., when a shopping game was added to the shopping section, usage and satisfaction increased. In this sense, it may be more appropriate to boost the "killer attributes" of each content category rather than to search for "killer applications."

Service providers

The broad mix of service providers in the ITV arena—cable operators, telephone and computer companies, movie studios, traditional broadcast networks, etc.—may lead to different mixes of services for consumers. There are strong differences in service philosophies among these groups as well as alternative assumptions about what consumers want. These differences are apparent in discussions by service groups about what they will provide. Many traditional broadcasters and cable channels see interactive television as a way for consumers to have more choice and control over what they view; some computer companies perceive ITV as a video database; and many telephone companies believe that communication should be an integral component in ITV services. Indeed, many telephone companies have struggled with the concept of program content. It has not been part of their corporate culture. The telephone after all does not have content. Content is created by the behavior of people who use the telephone.

New content raises the question of cost. Original interactive programming will be expensive. In a start-up phase, program providers have been reluctant to invest heavily in original content that can be used by a relatively small number of viewers. At the same time, some programming can be adapted to interactive formats with only modest increases in production costs. These include news, sports and game shows. However, original content will be required to fully exploit the new medium. Who will provide this? Also, will experimentation lead to any radical new program formats?

Advertising

Advertising may play a crucial role in the development of interactive television but its role is far from resolved. The first question that needs to be asked is how do we evaluate ITV as an advertising medium? Will interactive television serve as a traditional mass audience advertising medium or as a response/telemarketing medium? Two important characteristics of interactive television are the ability to segment audiences (providing different content to different audience segments and/or knowing which audience segments are watching) and to provide instantaneous feedback from audiences, including the direct purchase of products and services. These characteristics may lead system operators to charge advertisers in new ways, including a percentage of sales. Most likely, however, a hybrid model will emerge in which interactive television serves as a traditional mass medium for some applications and a telemarketing medium for others.

A second question concerns how consumers will respond to ITV commercials. Interactive television commercials can provide many new features for advertisers and consumers alike. For example, consumers could choose which commercial they wish to watch or which version of a commercial to watch. Commercials can offer contests in which a viewer might learn instantly if they have won a prize. Also, consumers can request additional information, instantly, or actually make a purchase during a commercial.

These features may make commercials more appealing to viewers and potentially reduce channel switching behavior during spots. However, there will undoubtedly be a novelty effect with these new forms of commercials. The important issue to research will be the behavior of viewers after any novelty effects have worn off.

A third issue is how will interactive television advertising be affected by other trends in advertising? There are many technological and behavioral changes taking place in television, e.g., the development of mega-channel cable television systems, menu driven user interfaces for television in which viewers can navigate through large capacity cable TV systems or program a VCR, and increased channel changing by viewers. The design and placement of commercials has been affected by these trends, e.g., many stations and networks no longer place commercials at the end of local news shows and simply cut directly to the opening of network news in order to reduce channel changing at this break point. This is called a "hot switch" or "seamless programming".

The development of interactive commercials will take place in a context of all these other technological and behavioral changes. Can interactive commercials serve some existing needs, e.g., reduce channel changing during commercials? Further, can interactive commercials provide a new setting in which advertisers can develop new formats that would be difficult to introduce in a traditional setting? For example, the development of specialized cable channels has provided a new setting in which it was possible to place program content and a commercial message on the same screen. This would be much more difficult to do in a broadcast network program, simply because a tradition has been established by which content and commercials are separated. Interactive programming may provide another new setting to explore new forms of advertising that would break traditions and expectations of broadcast and cable program settings.

The consumer

Do consumers want to interact with television? Interactive television contradicts the "couch potato" stereotype of television viewers. If television viewers are so passive, what interest would they have in interacting with television programs? Of course, the couch potato stereotype is a disputed concept. Some researchers argue that TV viewers have always responded, directly or indirectly, to what they view. Further, there are many examples of viewers responding in large numbers to interactive telephone response polls in news programming and after major political speeches. In addition, the well-documented channel changing behavior of many viewers may be considered a simple form of interacting with television [1].

Nonetheless, the basic question of mass consumer appetite for interactive television remains unanswered. Looking over a few decades of research on interactive television, it appears that consumer appetite for interactivity has grown and that there is a strong potential demand. However, there has yet to be a market trial or service with a robust offering of high-end ITV services.

What differences will we find among demographic groups? Will gender differences that have been found in other interactive technologies carry over to ITV [2]. Will usage skew towards younger audiences? A related question concerns ability to maneuver through interactive systems. Will viewers who have experience with personal computers and automated teller machines find interactive television easier to use than those who do not have experience with other interactive technologies?

What will consumers pay for interactive television? For planning purposes Bell Atlantic has indicated that it expects consumers to pay $55 per month for video services [7]. SW Bell expects combined spending for cable and telephone service to be in the $100–110 per month range [8]. This is higher than current expenditures but not necessarily unrealistic if consumers displace some of the money they now spend on videocassette rentals and move it over to the household ITV budget. The average household with cable TV, a VCR and telephone service spends approximately $120 on all three of these services combined. Further, some households spend considerably more per month. Presumably, early adopters of ITV would be those households with higher income and higher video spending patterns.

References

1. R. Bellamy and J. Walker, Television and the Remote Control, The Guilford Press: New York, pp. 44–46, 1996.
2. W. Bulkeley, "A tool for women, a toy for men: Gender affects how user sees the computer," and Joseph Pereira, "Video games help boys get a head start," The Wall Street Journal, p. B1, March 16, 1994.
3. W. Bulkeley and J. Wilke, "Can the exalted vision become reality," The Wall Street Journal, p. B1, Oct. 14, 1993.
4. W. Bulkeley and J. Wilke, op. cit., p. B1.
5. D. Cerverka, "Lessons learned from ITV trials," CED, pp. 38–42, May 1996.

6. F. Gerin and N. de Tavernost, "Biarritz and the future of videocommunications," in Wired Cities: Shaping The Future of Communications, William Dutton et al. (Eds.), G.K. Hall & Co., Boston, pp. 237–254, 1987.
7. K. Gibbons, "Bell Atlantic names vendors for video," Multichannel News, p. 1, May 23, 1994.
8. ———, (No title) CableWorld, p. 14, May 30, 1994.
9. V. Grosso, "AT&T's experiences with interactive television," presentation at The Twenty-Third Annual Telecommunication Policy Research Conference, Oct. 1, 1995.
10. H. Jessel, "Warning flags over VOD," Broadcasting and Cable, p. 33, March 20, 1995.
11. J. Keller, "AT&T's secret multimedia trials offer clues to capturing interactive audiences," The Wall Street Journal, p. B1, July 28, 1993.
12. J. Lipman, "Tuning out the TV of tomorrow," The Los Angeles Times, p. A1, Aug. 31, 1993.
13. K. Maney, "Interactive TV shows well in test drive." USA Today, p. 4B, Sept. 19, 1996.
14. S. McCarthy, "What time inc. learned," in Electronic Publishing Plus, Martin Greenberger (Ed.), White Plains, NY, Knowledge Industry Publications, pp. 163–168, 1985.
15. ———, A Summary Version of the Comprehensive Report On Hi-Ovis Project, New Media Development Association: Tokyo, 1988.
16. K. Mitchell, "Some boffo Bell Atlantic buy rates," Cable World, p. 20, March 25, 1996.
17. A.M. Noll and J. Woods, Jr., "The use of picturephone service in a hospital," Telecommunications Policy, pp. 29–36, March 1979.
18. M. Robichaux, "TV stations urged to go interactive," Broadcasting and Cable, p. 50, Dec. 20, 1993.
19. ———, "Innovative startup flops, and a lawsuit against TCI follows," The Wall Street Journal, p. A1, Feb. 26, 1995.
20. J. Schenker, "Interactive television keeps waiting to click with viewers," The Wall Street Journal Interactive Edition, Sept. 2, 1996.
21. "Symposium on experiments in interactive cable TV," Journal Of Communication, Vol. 28, No. 2, Spring 1978.

John Carey is Director of Greystone Communications, a telecommunications research and planning firm that he founded in 1980. He conducts planning, usability and marketing studies for new telecommunication services directed towards homes and businesses.

Clients have included American Express, AT&T, Bell Atlantic, CableVision, Consumer Reports, Continental Cablevision, Corporation for Public Broadcasting, Fidelity Investments, General Electric, National Exchange, The New York Times, NYNEX, Ogilvy and Mather, PBS, Prodigy, US Department of Commerce, WGBH TV, WNET TV, and Union Carbide, among others.

John is also an Affiliated Research Fellow at the Columbia Institute For Tele-Information in the Graduate School of Business at Columbia University and a consultant to the Freedom Forum Media Studies Center. Previously, he was a professor in the Interactive Telecommunications Program at New York University. He holds a Ph.D. in communications from the University of Pennsylvania and is the author of more than 50 publications on new media services and the adoption of telecommunication technology in homes and businesses.

Multimedia Tools and Applications 5, 217–222 (1997)

From Interactive Television to Internet Applications

GARY GLENN HARTWICK
Viacom, 1515 Broadway, New York, New York 10036

Abstract. Early in 1993 Viacom and a major telephony carrier formed a joint venture to trial interactive television (ITV) in Castro Valley, California. During the fall of 1994, it was decided not to complete this trial. Both companies decided, given what had already been learned planning for the ITV trial and the emerging strength of the Internet and the World Wide Web, that it would be more effective to focus on CD-ROMs, proprietary on-line services, and the Internet, including the World Wide Web, where many of the interactive applications that had been planned for ITV could be actually implemented and made available to large numbers of users. This paper discusses the interactive systems, and economic environments along with major issues, intellectual property rights, and Viacom's current direction.

Keywords: interactive television, video on demand, internet, interactive applications, content, on-line, content economics, intellectual property rights, World Wide Web, Castro Valley Trial, Viacom

Introduction

Early in 1993 Viacom and a major telephony carrier formed a joint venture to trial interactive television (ITV) in Castro Valley, California. The trial had a number of objectives including: 1) rebuilding the Castro Valley cable plant to 1 GHz with 500 home nodes to support emerging applications and services; 2) understanding markets for interactive services, consumer behavior, and applications such as video on demand, near video on demand, electronic programming guides, home shopping, games, travel services; and, 3) learning, developing, and implementing technologies such as compression, MPEG-2, transmission systems, video servers, set top boxes, remote control units, and operations systems.

During the fall of 1994, it was decided to review the need to complete this trial. Both companies decided, given what had already been learned planning for the ITV trial and the emerging strength of the Internet and the World Wide Web, that it would be more effective to focus on CD-ROMs, proprietary on-line services, and the Internet, including the World Wide Web. Most of the interactive applications that had been planned for the ITV trial could be actually implemented and made available to large numbers users in these environments. Many of the original objectives of the interactive television trial, to learn about markets, consumers, applications, and technologies for interactive services, have been met by these activities, and at much less cost to the company. The 1 GHz upgrade of the cable plant allowed Viacom to become a successful pioneer with cable modem technology and applications for the developing Internet and the World Wide Web.

The interactive environment

Viacom, though, is still in the process of defining interactive entertainment in an on-line[1] environment, an environment that both celebrates community and facilitates communication among individuals. Unlike more traditional forms of passive entertainment, interactive programming makes the user an integral part of the content. The emergence of this worldwide vehicle for communications and entertainment is leading to the creation of new forms of entertainment linking communities of people with similar interests. And that, in turn, is leading to opportunities for entertainment companies to extend their brands.

Today, though, nobody still has complete answers about what consumers want, need, and will pay for. Questions abound about the market size and the source of revenue. Functionality is an issue to be grappled with. The ultimate size of the user base can only be guessed at. All of these unknowns make the investment risk high.

At Viacom, the development of an interactive programming strategy has meant filtering out the hype from the hypertext, and this paper shares some of our thoughts and findings. It also describes briefly what Viacom, with its unique blend of brands such as MTV, Nickelodeon, Blockbuster, Simon & Schuster, and Paramount, is doing to understand the risk, to develop strategies, to manage them, and to position the company for continuing success. The promise of on-line services is too real, the potential too big, for anyone to walk away from it. But, serious issues beg to be resolved, issues such as the role of government, the question of international connectivity, and the question of privacy. There remain questions about what economic model or models will support the costs.

Right now there are four distinct ways companies can make money in this consumer marketplace: there is 1) the opportunity to sell equipment; 2) the opportunity to sell infrastructure; 3) the opportunity to provide security; and, 4) the opportunity to develop, provide, and support content.

Consumers are already footing the bill for connectivity in the home—90 percent of people buying new computers also buy modems. This major piece of enabling equipment is going into millions of homes yearly. Many companies are developing equipment and handling the sales. The Telecommunications Act of 1996 should help ensure that a competitive infrastructure will be built and maintained, and at costs that will presumably start falling. In the area of privacy and security, increasing attention is being paid to creating new, forward-looking means for protecting intellectual property and commercial transactions.

And that brings us to the fourth category—content. Viacom is a content company with interests in many different media delivered via many different platforms. For example:

- MTV: Music Television, the world's largest entertainment network, is available in 75 territories and 265 million homes worldwide.
- Simon & Schuster is the world's largest educational, computer book, and English-language book publisher.
- Paramount Pictures distributes its films in over 60 countries.
- Virgin Interactive Entertainment has distributed 100 game titles in over 30 countries.
- Paramount Canada's Wonderland hosts over 2.5 million guests annually.
- There are more than 65 million copies of Simon & Schuster's Star Trek books in print worldwide. Every minute, 13 Star Trek books are sold.
- Blockbuster Video has over 5,000 stores, with over 1,300 in 18 foreign markets, and plans to exceed 2,000 stores outside of the U.S. by the year 2000.
- Nickelodeon is seen in over 70 countries and 80 million households worldwide.
- A new Blockbuster store is opened somewhere in the world every 9 hours.

Viacom and all companies intending to participate in this new on-line environment must figure out what to do with and about content, and how to create a meaningful revenue source with it. However, this new on-line world is so high-tech that even before attention is turned to content, one must first deal with the systems required for its delivery.

The system environment

What is known? Consumers want television-type functionality with their on-line experience—instant-on, for example, plus the ability to change applications and services with the ease and speed of the television viewing experience. Unfortunately, the on-line industry's ability to fulfill cost-effectively these particular consumer desires is still wanting. The content industry and the consumer need speed. The content industry and the consumer need it cheap.

Signing on with a 28.8 modem may be better than signing on with the slower modems a majority of us are using now, but it is still light years away from the instant-on experience of television. Then there is ISDN, which has been lurking just around the corner for more than 10 years. But for the most part, it is still just a dream, not a reality. And even the potentially best of options, the cable modem, has a long way to go. Still to be resolved are return path and standards issues.

On-line industry revenues have been based on connect time, but the model is changing with competitive offers from long distance telephone companies, local exchange carriers, and cable companies. Proprietary on-line services may have to redefine their personality. Either they will move in the direction of content aggregators or, as more and more access providers offer cost-effective links to the Internet, they will have to lower their price.

Advertisers, too, are still experimenting with on-line services, and serious issues remain to be resolved regarding pricing structures and the establishment of meaningful tracking systems. While it is believed that advertising eventually will play a key role in driving mass deployment of on-line services and fuel the revenues supporting the creation of content, its contributions to the bottom line are unlikely to increase until there is some resolution of these issues. Merchandising transactions also account for a proportion of current on-line revenues.

But the consumer on-line shopping experience needs to improve. Catalogue-quality functionality was added over the past year, but it still does not compare with television shopping. The demographics also need to change to include more females. And, more efficient search engines that can help consumers locate what they want at the price they want to pay are needed.

The economic environment

It seems that the more traditional entertainment economic models do not translate easily to this new medium. For example: evaluate the costs to produce a once-a-week sitcom, say "Frasier". It is somewhere north of half a million dollars per episode. If 65 episodes are made, we are talking about $33 million. With the promise of potentially reaching 92 million domestic television households, significant backend revenues from syndication sales, in addition to the license fee from the television network, who in turn gets money from the advertising they sell, are generated. And, international sales are another source of revenue. So, clearly, the backend is what makes investment worthwhile.

But there is no backend equivalent for on-line. Given the interactive quality of the content, entertainment companies could be producing live programming all day, every day. Even allowing for economies of technology and scale, it would cost a fortune to program the equivalent of a prime-time schedule. Even with a potential 50 million modem household market by 1999, the numbers do not work. The logical conclusion, then, is that the creation of interactive entertainment cannot be supported by the same economic model. Also, given its nature, interactive content cannot simply be "repurposed" material, or even a digital version of what is now seen on television.

Viacom believes that real business success will come from understanding that digital entertainment should take advantage of what on-line does best, which is to connect people with common interests who want to communicate, to play together. It calls for a hybrid approach between today's packaged goods publishers and the on-line environment. For instance, CD-ROM or DVD based multiplayer games may have an on-line component. Also, in the fields of reference or education, a disk may be supplemented with updated on-line material.

All of these examples define the basic strategy: the global strengths of the brands should be extended across multiple platforms.

Intellectual property

Viacom is "technology indifferent," which gives it great freedom to explore actively ways to extend brands and franchises into all kinds of media. The "ubiquity model" followed puts product anywhere and everywhere that makes sense.

It should be noted, however, that content companies are extremely selective in placing content on-line because there are no effective protections in place for intellectual property. For all content providers, it is critical to ensure that rightsholders are appropriately paid for reproduction of their property. Until there is a safe, accurate, and fair method to track and compensate for use of materials, they are being extremely careful. As an intellectual property rights creator, Viacom is vigorous about copyright protection and enforcement. Copyright protection is a complex, centuries-old body of legislation and judicial opinion that balances creative and consumer rights. Intellectual property protection is essential to the availability of valuable content in a digital age.

Current direction

Currently, Viacom has over 45 web and proprietary on-line sites. Unlike several other content companies, product has not been aggregated under one giant web site, at least yet. Why yet—because the on-line medium today is about communications between people with similar interests. However, each business unit should decide how best to extend its own brands and franchises to the appropriate demographic target. Some initiatives directly bring in revenue, while others are designed more for promotional purposes. In any case, it is Nickelodeon who decides how best to extend the Nickelodeon brand; MTV, the MTV brand; Blockbuster, the Blockbuster brand, and so on. In essence, what is done with the on-line sites is no different than what is done in all other aspects of the business: strong targeting of the audience. Four examples are Paramount Pictures, Simon & Schuster, MTV, and Blockbuster.

Paramount Pictures established Paramount Digital Entertainment in May of 1995 with several major goals in mind, the first and foremost being to produce original interactive content that could make its way upstream to television and film. Paramount Digital Entertainment is exploring a number of exciting areas, not just in promotion and marketing, but also in forging partnerships with advertisers.

Simon & Schuster is also deep into on-line ventures. They view technology as an instrument for leveraging editorial and marketing content to educate, entertain, and inform. As a holder of 350,000 copyrights, Simon & Schuster uses on-line services for marketing, promotion, and publishing. Those 350,000 copyrights also make Simon & Schuster a key advocate for increased protection of intellectual property. Through Simon & Schuster's Macmillan Information SuperLibrary, the company is exploring how to sell books in an on-line world. The SuperLibrary features 15,000 pages of information containing 6,000 CD-ROMs and book titles, plus sample chapters. In reference publishing, it offers products such as "Arthur Frommer's Travel," which supplies travel information through Expressnet, a partnership between American Express and AOL. It is a high-tech way of expanding the classic travel series' services and readership.

On the entertainment front, MTV revamped its on-line look, adding new graphic interfaces and experiences, as well as original programming. Their lineup, "MTV Prime Time On-Line," was introduced featuring a nightly hour of original programming designed to create a true interactive experience. MTV continues to look at ways to marry on-line with on-air. For example, recently the channel went live "on-air" with a Red Hot Chili Peppers concert and also set up a live backstage chat with the band before the concert. MTV also has a live chat area known as YAK that occurs simultaneously on both MTV's cable feed and its on-line site. Participants can see each others' text onscreen on the on-line site, or can watch the cable channel and see both the text and random videos onscreen at the same time. MTV On-Line is not an extension of MTV. It is an innovative experience with its own personality, and its own identity.

Blockbuster is exploring online's potential as an alternate distribution channel. The Blockbuster music site is linked with the MTV and VH-1 sites. Users may choose from a list of available music, sample audio selections, and purchase CD's and cassettes using their credit cards. Blockbuster Video's site on the web is presently used for promotional activities. Just recently, the site allowed visitors to vote for their favorite entertainer in preparation for the Blockbuster Entertainment Awards show. Later this year, the site will be expanded to include Blockbuster video store content.

Conclusion

These, then, are the current thoughts, plans, and actions at Viacom. Viacom's interactive programming strategy is to proceed with caution and enthusiasm, placing our bet on content, not specific technology or platforms. In general "on-line" in this paper refers to proprietary on-line services, the Internet, and the World Wide Web. On-line services such as AOL, CompuServe, etc., are referred to as proprietary on-line services.

Note

1. In general "on-line" in this paper refers to proprietary on-line services, the Internet, and the World Wide Web. On-line services such as AOL. CompuServe, etc. are referred to as "proprietary on-line services."

Gary Glenn Hartwick is Vice President, Technology and Operations, Viacom Inc. As VP of Technology and Operations, Mr. Hartwick works to apply current and emerging technologies that help create and deliver entertainment and information services across Viacom's operating segments. Prior to the sale of Viacom Cable he was the Viacom Technical Liaison for the Castro Valley ITV trial. In addition, he is the Vice Chairman of the DAVIC Security Technical Committee and is a member of the Board of Editors of the SMPTE Journal.

MIX
Papier aus verantwortungsvollen Quellen
Paper from responsible sources
FSC® C105338

If you have any concerns about our products,
you can contact us on
ProductSafety@springernature.com

In case Publisher is established outside the EU,
the EU authorized representative is:
Springer Nature Customer Service Center GmbH
Europaplatz 3, 69115 Heidelberg, Germany

Printed by Libri Plureos GmbH
in Hamburg, Germany